"A brilliant exposition of how Bernie led hi[
to nowhere. A blistering, infuriating, and t[
— Andrew Cockburn, author *Kill Chain*

"Jeffrey St. Clair dissects the rotting, sold-out Democrats like no one since
Hunter Thompson, with encyclopedic insights and memory, and a sharp
surgical instrument that keeps the blood flowing. He pegged the progressive
Saint Bernie Sanders (and his Our Revolution schtick) as a paltry poser
and Hillary loyalist from day one, unlike the man's army of delusionary
worshippers. St. Clair's blow by blow coverage of the Democrats' insanely
orchestrated four day coronation of Wall Street Queen Hillary is by itself
worth the price of admission. *Fear and Loathing on The Campaign Trail*
thrives; buy the book, take the ride."

— John Stauber, author *Toxic Sludge Is Good For You*

"Caught between a vulgar talking yam and a vanquished 'Political
Revolution,' Jeffrey St. Clair slices through the muck and hype of the 2016
election with unique precision, skewering Donald Trump for his wreck-
ing-ball racism as much as he lacerates Bernie Sanders for bending knee
at the Democratic Party altar of Wall Street and war. St. Clair takes readers
on a boisterous romp through the political wreckage of the indispensable
nation, leaving shattered illusions in his wake, but always aiming toward
a principled populism as the only antidote to the spectacle suffocating the
American imagination."

— Arun Gupta, investigative journalist

"Movement reporting on a par with Mailer's *Armies of the Night.*"

— Peter Linebaugh, author of *Magna Carta Manifesto* & *Stop Thief!*

"The Democrats are now the war party, as Jeffrey St. Clair makes clear."

— Oliver Stone, director *Snowden*

"The Upton Sinclair of Oregon City."

— Jeff Baker, *The Oregonian*

"Jeffrey St. Clair is the Seymour Hersh of environmental journalism."

— Joshua Frank, author and journalist

Also by Jeffrey St. Clair

WHITEOUT: THE CIA, DRUGS AND THE PRESS
(with Alexander Cockburn)

A GUIDE TO ENVIRONMENTAL BAD GUYS
(with James Ridgeway)

BEEN BROWN SO LONG IT LOOKED LIKE GREEN TO ME

AL GORE: A USER'S MANUAL
(with Alexander Cockburn)

FIVE DAYS THAT SHOOK THE WORLD
(with Alexander Cockburn)

IMPERIAL CRUSADES: YUGOSLAVIA, AFGHANISTAN, IRAQ
(with Alexander Cockburn)

GRAND THEFT PENTAGON: TALES OF CORRUPTION IN THE WAR ON TERROR

RED STATE REBELS
(with Joshua Frank)

BORN UNDER A BAD SKY: NOTES FROM THE DARK SIDE OF THE EARTH

HOPELESS: BARACK OBAMA AND THE POLITICS OF ILLUSION
(with Joshua Frank)

KILLING TRAYVONS: AN ANTHOLOGY OF AMERICAN VIOLENCE
(with JoAnn Wypijewski and Kevin Alexander Gray)

BERNIE

& THE SANDERNISTAS

First published by
CounterPunch 2016

CounterPunch
PO Box 228
Petrolia, CA 95558

ISBN-13: 978-1539032724
ISBN-10: 1539032728

Library of Congress Control
Number: 2016955102

Designed by Tiffany Wardle

Typeset in Minion Pro, designed by
Robert Slimbach for Adobe Systems Inc.
and Founders Grotesk, designed by Kris
Sowersby for Klim Type Foundry.

BERNIE

& THE SANDERNISTAS

Field Notes From a Failed Revolution

JEFFREY ST. CLAIR

Table of Contents

**YOU SAY YOU WANT A REVOLUTION,
WELL, YOU KNOW....**

That Magic Feeling.. 1

**SEASON OF THE WITCH
ON THE CAMPAIGN TRAIL**

The Tale of the Birkenstock Bomber 13

St. Bernard and the Sandernistas 15

Bernie and the Jets 21

The Art of Trump l'Oeil Politics 25

When Chivalry Fails 29

A Comedy of Terrors 33

Blood Traces: Sanders and the Iraq War 37

Bully on the Bench.............. ,,,,,,,,   ,,,,   11

Hand Jobs: Heidegger, Hitler and Trump 45

The Candidate Who Came in From the Cold.............. 47

Good as Goldman 53

The Once and Future Sandernistas 57

**A PUBLIC BERNING
IMPROVISED NOTES FROM THE
DEMOCRATIC CONVENTION**

Day One: Don't Cry for Me DNC......................... 65

Day Two: The Humiliation Games....................... 73

Day Three: Night of the Hollow Men..................... 81

Day Four: She Stoops to Conquer 91

**THE END,
OF OUR ELABORATE PLANS,
THE END**

Bernie's Last Tape.. 105

Gratis 111

Index 113

YOU SAY YOU WANT A REVOLUTION, WELL, YOU KNOW....

That Magic Feeling

> Out of college, money spent
> See no future, pay no rent
> All the money's gone, nowhere to go
> Any jobber got the sack
> Monday morning, turning back
> Yellow lorry slow, nowhere to go
> But oh, that magic feeling…
> — Lennon and McCartney,
> *You Never Give Me Your Money*

BERNIE SANDERS HAD COME HOME. HOME TO NEW YORK. HOME to the city that fit his accent. Home to the borough that suited his cranky demeanor, his Jewish heritage, his gritty politics. Bernie Sanders wasn't Clean Gene McCarthy. Sanders is tightly wound. He could be petulant, moody, combustive. A little bit of Brooklyn was still hardwired into his character. Frankly, Sanders always seemed like an interloper in Vermont. Too prickly, urban and disputatious for that verdant and mountainous sliver of WASPish New England. If more of the Brooklyn Bernie had leaked out during the campaign, things might have ended differently.

On a cool night in early April, Bernie stood on the stage in Prospect Park, facing more than 28,000 adoring fans, the largest gathering of the campaign. As he worked his way through his speech, Sanders hit all of the familiar notes—on the minimum wage, single payer health care, free college tuition, the corrosiveness of Super PACS—but he stood a little taller, his voice sounded a little friskier, he seemed fueled by the sense that he just might win the New York primary.

Could New York really be in play? Could Sanders upend the once invulnerable Hillary Clinton in her own adopted state, sending shockwaves through the System? What once seemed impossible now seemed to many Sandernistas tantalizingly within grasp.

This was, of course, the season of the improbable, the rare warping of political time when the odds were being defied week after startling week. This was a primary season in which aliens and the alienated finally featured in guest-starring roles. The mood of the country, sour and aggravated, seemed primed to embrace, for the first time in decades, a real outsider candidate, not so much because they found either of the two self-identified outsiders especially alluring, but because the electorate saw themselves as outsiders, exiles from a political system run by and for a remote and untouchable cabal of corporations, militarists and financial elites.

Nearly all agreed the system was rigged, programmed like some political malware to replicate the same results over and over again, generating torrents of booty into fewer and fewer hands, while leaving the rest of the Republic mired in debt and endless war.

Indeed, war has become the nation's permanent condition. There seems to be a new one every few months. Few can keep up. And who goes off to fight them? Not many of us, or even people that we know. A new warrior class seemed to have taken root. We noticed them mainly from the decals on their trucks or from their wheelchairs and prosthetic limbs, rarely encountered in the check out line at Safeway.

More and more, machines were doing the war's wetwork, killing nameless people in nameless regions on the far side of the world, hundreds of miles from any known base of operations. War has become background noise, the ambient soundtrack of our time.

It is one of the great failures of the Sanders campaign that he didn't try to puncture some of the comforting illusions about American foreign policy. As cruelly as we treat our own citizens, Americans like to believe, in fact *must* believe, that our country remains a force of light and goodness in the most troubled precincts of the world. We are reluctant warriors, heroes for humanity. Sanders had a rare chance to expose America's savage imprint on the world to his followers. With more than 800 military bases sprawling across the globe, the American military machine keeps the unruly living under a constant state of nuclear terror, each transgression against the imperial order disciplined and punished by SEAL team assassins, cruise missiles and drone strikes out of the clear blue skies.

The financial condition of the country also seems mired in a mysterious contradiction. The number of billionaires doubles every year, while everyone else is working harder yet falling behind month by month. In fact, the economy, chronically ailing for so long, finally seems to have turned malignant. Everybody knows this. Even the looters. Especially them. And the government is useless. Worse than useless. It exists not to contain the spread of economic disease or to alleviate the suffering, but to repress any minor revolt of the afflicted cells of the Republic. The evidence is all around. In homeless shelters, tent cities, food banks, and unemployment offices. Or under lock and key. One in 31 adults in America is rotting in prison or jail, or living circumscribed lives on probation or parole. Twenty-five years ago, this rate was only 1 in 77. Police are killing a citizen somewhere on the streets of America every 12 hours or so, and every 18 hours that citizen is a black male. In fact, in the first six months of 2016 police had killed 585 people, up from the previous year's total of 491 killed through June of 2015.

The country is out of joint. It had been for a long time. Was it really possible that the sleepers had awakened? That Tea Partiers and Occupiers, Steelworkers and Black Lives Matter activists, had experienced a simultaneous epiphany? That some kind of convulsive change in the old corrupt orthodoxy was just around the corner? Well, so it seemed to some of us, suckers for almost any wish-fulfillment fantasy, in the crazy winter of discontent in America, circa 2016.

Until that rare flash in New York, Bernie Sanders had largely refused to engage Clinton directly. But in the first real skirmish of the campaign, Sanders indelicately declared that Clinton was disqualified from holding the presidency for taking money from Wall Street and for voting to give George W. Bush the authority to go to war in Iraq. Sanders had finally landed a blow that seemed to stagger Clinton. But it was a parry-and-thrust that Bernie retreated from almost immediately after being hit with a cluster bombing of attacks by Hillary's praetorian guard of liberal pundits and DNC hacks.

But if Bernie's blitz through New York was a time of swelling optimism for his campaign, it was also a moment of peak delusion. Bernie had lost the nomination well before he ended up losing New York, in something of a Clinton rout. In fact, the campaign had been over since Super Tuesday, when HRC marched almost unopposed across the South, racking up an insurmountable delegate lead. But the Revolution was defunct the moment Sanders elected to run as a Democrat, a decision he doubled down on months later when he rebuffed Jill Stein's offer to the head the Green Party ticket and chose to endorse Hillary Clinton without equivocation on Prime Time TV at the Democratic Convention in Philadelphia.

That fateful decision left a pall of evil hanging over the elections. A palpable evil. An evil you could smell. Even many of Hillary's backers knew she was a force of evil. It's why they talked so openly and frantically about the logic of *lesser* evil voting.

They knew she couldn't be trusted. That whatever Faustian deal she struck with Sanders would not be honored. They knew that Clinton lies smoothly, effortlessly, and icily. That she lies about big and small matters, from her Goldman speeches to TPP, from her personal finances to Libya, from her e-mails to the DNC's plot to get Bernie. Yes, even Democratic Party loyalists acknowledged her evil ways. But could they really be sure, deep down, that she was truly the lesser evil? What kind of complex calculus yielded the proof?

For the Democrats, the greater evil was Donald Trump, who seemed to rise like some monstrous dirigible on the same political air currents that had sent Sanders aloft. The two outsiders were in a sense alter egos, Sanders's Dr. Jekyll to Trump's Mr. Hyde. They spoke about many of the same issues, the same frustrations with the economic and political condition of the country, to strikingly different audiences and in different tones. Trump prevailed because he was willing, indeed eager to burn down the Republican Party house with him. Sanders failed, in large part, because he wasn't, even when the Democratic Party house, run with the ruthless calculation of any casino, conspired against him.

Trump burst on the scene like a character out of a Burroughs novel, a narcissistic junkie, desperate for his next fix of publicity—jittery, unpredictable, obscene, petulant and brutal. And impossible not to watch. There was a dark and dangerous erotic charge to Trump that was lacking in his rivals, especially from Sanders and Clinton, both of whom projected antiseptic and asexual personas. Trump, on the other hand, emitted the powerful pheromones of doom. At times it was hard to tell whether Trump was running a political campaign or directing a political snuff film.

At Sanders events all the erotic charge surged not from the candidate himself, but the from the energized crowds. His rallies were intense experiences that often felt like political raves. They vibrated, the crowds grooving to that magic feeling.

Hillary, naturally, projected the severe aridity of a tax auditor. Clinton's foot soldiers looked like an army of grim conscripts going off to wage battle against their own villages. HRC would prevail, but even her most devoted followers knew there would be no fun in the triumph. It seemed unlikely that she could chop down Trump—and for months polls showed Sanders as the better bigot-slayer—Hillary knew all along what she really had to do was wait, wait for Trump to self-destruct. Only Sanders could trip her up and she and the DNC had that unlikely prospect pretty much fixed from the start. She didn't need to be appealing. Clinton's calling card was her inevitability.

Trump has been called the new Goldwater. But Goldwater had a theory of the case, an ideology that was austere, formulaic and unyielding. Trump feeds off of rage. From his gold-plated aerie in Trump Tower, the Donald saw the circuits of the old white America shorting out, spraying sparks of anxiety and dread, fear and suspicion. These were the people who believed to their core that they had built America and that the country should put their economic security first. And now they found themselves just scraping by at the end of most months on pay day loans and pawn shops. They were pissed off and they were looking for someone to blame. And Trump fed off their rage like a super villain prowling the streets of Gotham City. His ideology is a pastiche of raging factions: on trade, on immigration, on race, on sexual insecurity, on their incandescent fury at the elites. Not surprisingly, Trump rallies often erupted into spasms of virulent, profane shouting.

Sanders was probing other emotional states. He seemed to play the role of analyst or counselor, an antidote to the despair, alienation and the hopelessness of America's abandoned children. Sanders rallies—much larger and younger than Trump's crowd—often left in tears, ecstatic tears, as if the crowds had gone through a kind of collective psychodrama and emerged purged, emotionally spent. It was as if the Sandernistas had finally found someone who "got them," who heard and felt their laments and gave voice to their longing for connection.

One can see what the Sandernistas were getting out of being part of Bernie's movement: the thrill of collective action, the buzz of being in the midst of a tumultuous, even slightly dangerous political force. But what about Sanders himself? What compelled Bernie Sanders, at his age, to keep up the grueling grind of the campaign, especially when he knew (and he had to know, didn't he?) how it was all going to end? Validation for decades of work? Ego gratification? Did he labor under any guilt for leading his bright young legions of believers right into the dark vaults of the neoliberal machine they'd been warring against? Or in Bernie's mind was that, to use James Baldwin's phrase, just the price of the ticket for the wild trip he'd taken them on? Hard to say. At a personal level, Sanders remains opaque, inscrutable. Politically, he sticks rigidly to his old script, even long after the point when his performances have entered into reruns.

Where Trump breathes fire, Sanders often exhales a kind of sourness, emblematic, perhaps, of the unpalatable nature of the political machine he found himself locked inside of. Sanders ended up a prisoner of his politics, of his fatal decision to run inside the Democratic Party instead of against it. Sanders offered revolution, but the targets of the revolution could never be precisely stated. The beast could not be named, because it had been inculcated, reared and unleashed on the nation by his very own party. So it often seemed as if Sanders was speaking in a kind of code. Indeed as the campaign went on, one began to hope that he was speaking in code, that there was a subliminal dimension to his rhetoric that was being picked up and deciphered by an underground movement ready to rise up against the unnamed enemy—neoliberalism—and its chief practitioners: Obama and the Clintons. But, alas, it was not to be.

Sanders's losing campaign, a campaign fated to lose, was not a campaign that attracted losers, not even beautiful losers. By and large, the Sandernistas were not social outcasts, not the homeless, the marginalized and the downtrodden. They weren't black or Chicano. No. The Sandernistas were not scruffy street urchins and Bernie Sanders was not our political Dickens. They were raised in the suburbs of Madison and Denver on the white bread virtues of the old American Dream, a promise that had evaporated before their very eyes. They were educated and vested in the System, with enough social and economic status to have a credit score and acquire a mound of debt. The challenge for the Sandernistas will be to get beyond their sense of personal and political betrayal and to finally connect their movement for revolutionary change with the long-standing grievances of the American underclass.

In the end, Trump proved to be something of a superficial storm, a dusty twister, ripping across the surface of the country, leaving only minor structural damage in its wake. Sanders, though, seemed to be tapping into some deeper strata, down into the psychic fault lines of the nation, probing hidden fractures that might shift and quake at any moment. Yet the senator seemed insensate to the exact nature of the political and emotional schisms his campaign had helped expose. As the weeks went on, the fervency of his crowds swelled, yet Sanders seemed not to notice the expectant mood, the palpable yearning of his adherents. He kept giving the same stump speech at event after event, numb to the hunger of the beast he had awakened. In a weird way, Sanders and Trump ended up sharing one more attribute as outsider politicians. Ultimately, their campaigns proved to be more about the candidates themselves than any great political principle or ideological crusade.

Where Trump blustered about "making America great again," Sanders actually presented himself, symbolically at least, as being from a time when America thought of itself not only as great but also as good. Sanders stood behind his podium like a kind of Old Testament embodiment of the rapidly eroding Codes of the New Deal and the Great Society. In an age of accelerating national anxiety, the metaphysical promise of Bernie Sanders seemed to be that perhaps America could at least be humane.

But as the election proved, it's a thin line between hope and hate. If Trump acted like an existential pest, a confidence man manipulating the basic impulses of a Hobbesian mob, Sanders offered, in his opaque manner, the soothing notion that the rusty gears of a long-neglected government machine could still be retooled to comfort and uplift. In this way, he revealed that he really was an antiquated Democrat, preaching socialism for a collapsing middle class.

Here then was the key to unlock the appeal of Bernie Sanders and his ultimate failure. At one of those rare, epochal moments, when the nation, preoccupied by the nature of its identity and obsessed with its engagement with the world, seemed to be searching desperately for a new logic to its existence, Sanders was punching a collective ticket back to a past that never existed.

What follows is a real-time chronicle of a failed revolution, a portrait of a movement which sparked to life and flared brightly for 10 months before being snuffed out by its strange and stubborn leader, a man who proved unworthy of his most devoted followers.

— *August 10, 2016*

SEASON OF THE WITCH
ON THE CAMPAIGN TRAIL

The Tale of the Birkenstock Bomber

THE MOST USEFUL PARABLE ABOUT PROGRESSIVES IS THAT OFFERED by Bernard Sanders, the self-styled "socialist-progressive-independent" representative from Vermont. Sanders owes his political career to the radicals' rage against the Vietnam War, many of whom moved into Vermont in the early '70's and subsequently planned a long-term, carefully organized assault on Vermont's two-party structure by organizing a third force, the Progressive Alliance. Sanders linked his political ambitions to this effort, became mayor of Burlington and, later, congressman.

At a rapid pace, his emphasis moved from party-building to Sanders-building. By 1994, it was apparent that the only movement in which Sanders was interested, was the movement of liberal money into his political campaign trough. One piece of opportunism followed another, always forgiven by Vermont *pwogressives* who were frightened of Sanders and feared to speak out against the loudmouth fraud, even though, in 1998, Sanders spoke vehemently in Congress in favor of sending his state's nuclear waste into a poor, largely Hispanic, township in Texas called Sierra Blanca.

Sanders supported sanctions against Iraq. Then he voted in favor of the war on Serbia: once, twice… and on April 28, 1999, he did it again. This was the astounding 213-213 tie vote, which meant that the House of Representatives repudiated the war on Serbia launched by Clinton in violation of Article One of the US Constitution., which reserves war-making powers to Congress.

So if the "socialist progressive" "anti-war" Sanders had voted in line with the anti-war sentiments he has forged a career upon, the result would have been even *a straight majority for the coalition of Republicans and radical Democrats.*

On April 26, 1999, even before his most recent vote of shame, Sanders' office was occupied by fifteen radical Vermonters sickened by his stance. The sit-in echoed the 1984 occupation of (Republican) Jim Jeffords' office in 1984 by the Winooski 44, protesting Reagan's war in Central America.

Jeffords waited three days before asking the police to remove the protesters. Sanders waited six hours.

A week later on May 3rd, Sanders held a town hall meeting in Monteplier attended by the fifteen protesters, wearing chains. The man in Sanders' Burlington office who told the protesters that Sanders wouldn't speak to them was Philip Fiermonte—ironically one of the original Winooski 44.

Readers of the *Washington Post's* first edition can be forgiven if they missed the historic House vote refusing to approve the bombings, tucked away coyly on page A27. *The New York Times* had a better sense of news and history and put the vote on its front page, above the fold: "Deadlocked House Denies Support for Air Campaign." *The Washington Times* had a front-page banner headline: "House Refuses to Back Air War on Serbs: Separate Vote Denise Funds for Deploying Ground Forces." In the Vietnam era it took years for resistance in the House to even approach that level. Too bad Sanders was on the side of the laptop bombers.

—with Alexander Cockburn.

— *June 5, 1999*

St. Bernard and the Sandernistas

> I'm going to be a happy idiot
> And struggle for the legal tender
> Where the ads take aim and lay their claim
> To the heart and the soul of the spender
> And believe in whatever may lie
> In those things that money can buy
> Though true love could have been a contender
> Are you there?
> Say a prayer for the Pretender
> Who started out so young and strong
> Only to surrender
> — Jackson Browne, *The Pretender*

I ADMIT IT. I HAD FINALLY BEGUN TO WARM TO BERNIE SANDERS. With each new Berniefest, the old animosities melted a little. After years of unmitigated loathing for Sanders, I was beginning to feel a little pride in the homespun campaign waged by the Faux Comrade from Vermont.

Much of this had to do with the creeping anxiety that Sanders and his growing band of 'Sandernistas', are inflicting on Hillary Clinton. Every time Hillary is forced to pop some political Prozac, a part of me cheers. Thank you, Bernie.

It's a curious appeal. I've never thought of Bernie Sanders as a spellbinding speaker. He doesn't have the polished allure of Obama or the seductive flair of Jesse Jackson in his prime. His Brooklyn accent is thick, his style more stentorian than passionate. The key to Bernie's charisma is his charming lack of it. But his stump speeches, offering a plodding pastiche of the same liberal economic platitudes that have been common currency since Hubert Humphrey, packed the masses in, from Denver to Madison. The seething desperation of the economic margins of the country lured people toward Sanders—the only antidote for their anguish.

In the presence of this largely *ad hoc* movement, it is almost possible to anesthetize one's conscience against the moral revulsion prompted by Sanders' adamantine allegiance to the Israeli state in the face of one atrocity after another. After all, nearly every politician in Washington acts like an automaton programed by the Lobby. One can also temporarily stifle one's distaste for his stubborn support of a blustery our-way-or-the-highway militarism, from Yemen to Ukraine. Likely it seemed the 'politic' 'thing' to do at the time.

The self-proclaimed Independent Socialist even initially backed Bill Clinton's cruel bombing campaign against Serbia, an 'independent socialist' country. Oh, well, the era of Post-Modernism has apparently given way to the age of Post-Irony. Sanders isn't a pacifist. Unlike most socialists (excepting, naturally, those of the Christopher Hitchens School of Neo-Trotskyist Interventionism), Sanders is not even an Anti-Imperialist. Understood. But did the senator have to go so far as to call in the cops to arrest anti-war protesters who had peaceably assembled at his office in Burlington? Tough call, I guess. Perhaps his staffers had dinner reservations at a hot new bistro in Brattleboro and needed to close up shop early that day.

One must, I suppose, tolerate Bernie's ongoing backing of a bloated military budget, especially for the production of fighter jets and aircraft carriers, because it means jobs for Vermonters. That's merely called 'bringing home the bacon' and all politicians do it, more or less.

Sweep aside, for a moment, Sanders' bewildering votes for draconian federal crime and anti-terror laws, even one that savagely eviscerated the right of *habeas corpus*, a minor infraction, apparently, which has hardly been noticed, even on this, the 800th anniversary, of Magna Carta.

The Sanders' campaign isn't attracting many black supporters to his super-rallies, and this is unfortunate. Perhaps this explains the senator's catatonic reaction in Phoenix when confronted by Black Lives Matters activists. He was, in the words of one of his backers, "ambushed." Almost certainly, he'll soon get his groove back and do better next time. Yet, it's easy to understand why so many African-Americans resist his charms. Where was he when they needed him? Where is he now, as the black body count continues to mount at the hands of the state?

These nagging caveats which keep percolating with the annoying persistence of Banquo's Ghost, can, with maximum effort, be suppressed for the over-riding goal of finally humiliating Hillary Clinton and the eradicating the toxic virus of Clintonism that has ravaged the political body of the American left for more than two decades. Yes, I confess! I'm an ABHer (pronounced "Abhor")—Anybody But Hillary. I mean *anybody*, even Martin (Who-the-Hell-is-That?) O'Malley. But Bernie suddenly, even miraculously, had the best shot. He was the one rattling the gilded cage, getting under her skin.

But here's the rub. Bernie had *no* plans to humiliate Hillary. He's been an accidental agent of her anxiety and he always intended to keep it that way. Bernie refused to go negative, and pledges to support the eventual nominee of the party—Hillary.

This restraint earned the senator the patronizing plaudits of Rachel Maddow and the Hipster Chorus at MS-DNC. *How refreshing*, they swoon. *At last, a politician who only wants to talk positively about the issues! No cynical attack ads! No nagging questions about Hillary's inexplicable enrichment in the commodities market! No unsettling inquiries into her support for the Iraq war or the illegal bombing of Libya. No nasty condemnations of Hillary's support for the dismantling of welfare or her cozy relations to the economic wrecking crew at Goldman, Sachs!* Bernie's going to keep it light and upbeat. He says he likes Hillary, respects her, doesn't want to besmirch the reputation of the presumptive nominee. Keeping it positive. Dig it.

But Bernie's disarmament strategy makes little sense, understood in the context of the political combat of contemporary presidential campaigns, where, in theory at least, the stakes are as high as they come. Sanders' non-aggression pact would never have been reciprocated by Hillary in the unlikely event that her now prohibitive lead began to shrink. The Clintons play gutter politics. Recall Bill's racist shivving of Obama during the 2008 primaries in South Carolina?

So, alas, Bernie and the Sandernistas have succeeded in squashing every little bit of enjoyment I had in his campaign. There's nothing like the rampaging delusions of acolytes, to reinvigorate the repressed hatred of a political realist.

I should have known better. There was that insistent voice in the back of my head with the familiar Anglo-Irish accent, the one saying: "Jeffrey, what's happened to your bullshit detector?" Yes, the shade of Alexander Cockburn, sometime summer resident of Vermont and longtime critic of Sanders' special brand of political impotence. "Bernie and the Pwogs," Alex snickered, "Really, Jeffrey, you're *slipping*."

And, of course, he's right. Pull the Sandersmobile into the garage for inspection, pop the hood and you'll soon discover the vacuous truth: no engine, just an exhaust pipe, pumping out rhetoric. So much talk, so little action. The deeper you look at Sanders, the less substance you see.

The real problem with Bernie is that he won't allow you to suffer illusions. Obama was a neophyte, with hardly any record, except the ominous warning signal that flashed when he picked Joe Lieberman as his senatorial mentor. It was easy to inhale the aroma of HOPE and become momentarily intoxicated. Bernie, in contrast, has a 40-year record as a politician. He is what he is. To say what he is, to state what he's done, is not to imitate Cassandra at the wall and predict the flames of the future. It's more akin to Tacitus combing through the dusty annals year after year: a politician who promises one thing and delivers, time and again, something else entirely.

These are the times when I wish the psycho-historians were still active to put the Liberal-Left onto the couch. The left-wing of the Democratic Party has been vilified since at least the Jackson campaign, but the decades of mistreatment by the party establishment only draws them tighter into the grip of their abusers. They are constantly on the hunt for 'The Good Father' and see him in the strangest incarnations: Dennis Kucinich, Mario Cuomo, Paul Wellstone, Barack Obama. They are so desperate to be accepted, to be loved, to be coddled, that they remain completely blind to the fact that they are about to be tasered back into submission.

The Democratic Party bought into neoliberalism with the election of Carter (they've always been imperialistic) and the sale was completed during Clinton time. Since then there's been no revolution or even minor rebellion inside the party. Even Bernie, the putative socialist, speaks fondly of the booming Clinton economy.

How can this party be saved? Why should it? Give Bernie credit for honesty—at least. Even as he pledges to return to the Senate as an Independent, he does so after finally admitting what he is: a Democrat with all the baggage that comes along with that membership card and his dedication to the election of HRC, the preeminent neoliberal politician in the world today.

Bernie has inherited the time-honored role of 'The Pretender', an essential character in Democratic Party stagecraft. There have been other Pretenders who have strutted and fretted their way across the primary season: Gene McCarthy and Shirley Chisholm, George McGovern and Jerry Brown, Cuomo and Jesse Jackson, Bill Bradley and Patricia Schroeder, Kucinich and, yes, even Barack Obama, the Pretender who became president.

Yet none of these insurgencies have moved the Democratic party even one micron to the left. Instead the DNC has lurched ever right. If nothing else, the Obama experience has demonstrated that the potency of the change agent dissolves almost instantly when dropped into the swells of the System.

The sole purpose of these insurgencies is to keep the Left locked inside of a party that no longer actively represents any of their interests. It's a sad and hopeless confinement, a kind of political life without parole. Sure, many of the Left's most cherished issues, from abortion rights to climate change, minimum wage to single-payer, get put "on the table" as a way to keep the backers of the losing campaign animated enough to vote in the general election. Some of these planks will even get inscribed into the Holy Writ of The Platform, where they will be promptly embalmed and entombed until the next convention.

Bernie Sanders had a choice. He could have run as the outsider he claimed to be. He could have run as an independent. He could have run as a Socialist or a Green. He could have been a threat to the *status quo*. But he wilted. Either because Sanders really is at heart a Democrat—or because he is a political coward who feared retribution, he gave credence to a party that has brutalized nearly every progressive policy he claims to champion.

Meanwhile, truly independent campaigns, the ones that forcefully challenge the neoliberal dogma and imperialistic militarism of the Democratic Party from the outside, are crushed, their candidates and supporters vilified and demonized. Go ask Ralph Nader.

— July 31, 2015

Bernie and the Jets

Hillary laid a political trap and Bernie Sanders, in his schlemiel-like way, stumbled right into it.

In the wake of Jeremy Corbyn's smashing victory as the new leader of Britain's Labour Party, Hillary's super-PAC, Correct the Record, tarred Sanders as a Corbyn-like renegade who had cozied up to untouchable figures like Hugo Chavez.

About a decade ago, Sanders was part of a delegation that negotiated a sensible deal to bring low-cost heating oil from Venezuela to poor families in the northeastern United States. But instead of defending his honorable role in this *ex parte* negotiation, Sanders wilted. In a fundraising email to his legions of Sandernistas, Bernie fumed at being "linked to a dead Communist dictator."

Of course, Hugo Chavez represented everything that Bernie Sanders claims to be. Chavez is an independent socialist whose immense popularity in his own country led to his Bolivarian Party winning 18 straight hotly-contested elections since 1996, not to mention surviving several coup attempts backed by the CIA and the editorial board of the *New York Times*, plots that elicited not a squeak of dissent from Bernie the Red.

One might be tempted to cut the Vermont senator some slack on the matter. After all, Sanders seems to have given foreign policy in the post-911 era about as much attention as he has police violence in urban American. As the American military skids into Syria, one looks to Sanders (who else is there?) for new ideas, for a holistic political philosophy that links neoliberal economics with racism and imperial adventurism. Yet we see nothing of the kind. How does Sanders feel about the latest war we've backed our way into in the Middle East? Who can really say? No one is sure if Sanders himself really knows, and this not merely because Bernie so often seems to be speaking in tongues, without even the spiritual uplift a Pentecostal sermon provides.

Sanders' core political ideas seem scrawled on parchment, as stale and faded as those of the American politician he most resembles, Hubert H. Humphrey. The country's most acerbic political journalist, Robert Sherrill, called Humphrey the Drugstore Liberal. The Minnesota Democrat was an economic populist, perhaps even to the Left of Sanders, who remained insensate to the horrors of the American war machine. Like Sanders, Humphrey directed almost all of his economic rhetoric at the middle class—what nearly everyone else in the world calls the *bourgeoisie*—a curious target demographic for an avowed socialist.

As the nation sank deeper into the blood of Vietnam, Humphrey's sole consolation was to dole out economic palliatives while talking up the number of high-paying jobs generated by the arms manufacturers. Like Humphrey, Sanders is a military Keynesian who seems to believe that the never-ending War on Terror is one sure-fire route toward full-employment. In other words, he's a Cold War Liberal lost in a post-Cold War world.

Still, Bernie clings to his death-dealing supersonic relics, most fervently to the F-35 Lightning II fighter jet. As Andrew Cockburn reported in *Harper's*, Sanders and his Vermont colleague Patrick Leahy waged a fierce bureaucratic fight to bring the jet to the Burlington Air Base as the premier weapon of the Green Mountain Boys, the 158th Fighter Wing of the Vermont Air National Guard. At $191 million per aircraft, the F-35 represents a technological wish-fulfillment for the defense lobby. Larded with the latest high-tech thanatic gizmos, the porcine and unstable Stealth fighter will prowl cloud-free skies (too dainty to fly in rain) on an endless quest to confront an enemy that no longer exists, and perhaps never did. The only people who will be terrorized by Bernie's fleet of F-35s (when they finally arrive) are the poor residents of South Burlington, whose homes will be perpetually quaking from the caterwauling squeal of the jet's after-burning turbofan engine. Indeed, the noise will be so disruption that more than 6,000 people may be forced to move out of their homes.

Award Bernie bonus points for consistency here. He is equally supportive of gun manufacturers, rejecting even the most timid restrictions on gun sales and voting to shield weapons-makers from liability suits brought by victims of mass shootings link. A few hours after the rampage at Umpqua Community College in Roseburg, Oregon, Bernie hypocritically tweeted out a statement of condolence for the victims which was notable only for the extreme banality of its sentiment.

Two days later, when U.S. airstrikes targeted a Doctors Without Borders hospital in Kunduz, Afghanistan, killing 22 medical workers and patients, Sanders's twitter-wire went tellingly mute. But what could Sanders say about this war crime in real time, an attack that infused a new meaning to the phrase 'surgical strike'? The miserable 14-year-long war on Afghanistan is the battle Sanders said had to be waged, a war without regrets.

Alexander Cockburn used to say that one of the pre-conditions for being a "serious presidential contender" was the ability to confess publicly, often live on *Meet the Press*, that you were willing to launch nuclear weapons against (pick a country, any country will do....), even at the risk of incinerating life on Earth.

Of course, these days, you also have to pledge support for Obama's drone killing program, as Bernie Sanders has faithfully done. Sanders told George Stephanopoulos in August that if he becomes the next joystick bombardier in the Oval Office, he won't pull the plug on the drones but he will endeavor to kill fewer innocent people. Rarely has the moral hollowness of American liberalism been expressed more clearly.

Thank you, Comrade Bernie.

— *November 13, 2015*

The Art of Trump l'Oeil Politics

1985. REAGAN HAS JUST BEEN REELECTED, BUT REPUBLICAN fortunes across the country are waning. The Gipper is beginning to show his incapacities and the party itself seem just as hoary. The hunt is on for new blood and George Clark, the chairman of the New York Republican Party, thinks he knows just the man to reno-vate the GOP: Donald Trump.

Clark rides the express elevator to Trump's penthouse on the top floor of Trump Tower, a kind of Versailles-in-the-Sky. The Republican powerbroker has a simple question to put to Trump: will the real estate titan consider running for governor against Mario Cuomo in 1987? Trump quickly answers. "No. President or nothing."

A disappointed Clark descends the 1,388-feet black monolith, perhaps thinking that Trump's decision was based on his entangle-ments with Cuomo, an icon of liberalism. As a young lawyer, Cuomo had represented Trump's father, Fred, in some of his sleaziest proj-ects. And when Cuomo ran for governor, the younger Trump was there to bankroll his campaign, certain that Cuomo would return the favors. He was not disappointed. The Cuomo administration interceded again and again on behalf of Trump projects, from the Television City development to the perennially embattled Grand Hyatt in New York. It is possible to trace Trump's view of the govern-ment as a kind of Ponzi scheme to be plundered for his own profit to this fruitful partnership with the Cuomo regime.

Indeed, Trump became so enamored with Cuomo that the magnate privately urged him to run for president. But why didn't Trump thrust himself into the 1988 campaign against Poppy Bush, a man he had ridiculed as a "waffling weakling"? According to Wayne Barrett's acidic must-read biography, *Trump: the Deals and the Downfall*, the Donald perceived that he was fatally weighted by a political liability: his Czech wife, the feisty Ivana. "Nobody in

South Carolina will like Ivana's accent," Trump told friends. "Plus, she's from a Communist country!" But Trump had a plan to polish his political appeal: dump Ivana and marry Marla Maples, a vapid beauty queen from Georgia. Trump confided to his bodyguard that Marla was the key element in his Southern Strategy. "They go wild for the glamour down there." Alas, it was not to be.

Now, twenty years, several bankruptcies and two failed marriages later, Donald Trump is back with a new Southern Strategy, which he unveiled in enervating detail at his Alabama Trumpalooza. It was the face of a new and perhaps even more unappetizing Trump, the billionaire populist. For decades, Donald Trump's persona was that of an upbeat pitchman, a huckster for the imperial dream of infinite growth, even when his own fortunes were flagging—especially then.

But now Trump's public mood has soured. His pitches have assumed a dark, fatalistic tenor. He sells fear and white rage, as if he has scented the rot eating away inexorably at the core of the System he helped construct. Of course, he still markets himself as the nation's top stud, the only figure man enough to eradicate the gravest threat to the Republic: Mexican immigrants.

Is Trump's noxious nativism an act, a case of Trump l'Oeil politics? Who knows, but it is certainly a grandiose hypocrisy. The family fortune was built on immigrant labor. His father Fred boasted that his empire of suburban shacks was constructed by laborers "right off the boat," untainted by union membership. Donald followed the same reasoning at his own construction sites and in the low-wage jobs at his casinos and hotels.

Donald Trump is a bigot and a pig who uses his boorishness to appeal to other pigs, his targeted demographic of second generation Reagan Democrats: white, blue-collar men, fueled by Budweiser, sexual insecurity and a roiling, if inchoate, resentment toward a political system that has pushed them to an economic cliff. It is a measure of Trump's mystique that these economic refugees are drawn fervently to a man who trademarked the phrase: "You're fired!"

I doubt Trump has read even a paragraph by Guy Debord, but his presidential campaign would thrill the Situationists. Trump for President is the Greatest Spectacle on Earth—or at least on Fox News. Who else has shredded Roger Ailes on his own network? What other Republican has defended single-payer health care? Derided Citizens' United? Inveighed against global trade pacts? Denounced the Iraq War as an act of unparalleled stupidity? Aggressively pushed a progressive taxation model? It's as if Trump has stepped right off the pages of Ralph Nader's Dickensian romp of a novel, *Only the Super-Rich Can Save Us!*

But is the Donald really a class traitor? Hardly. Trump is a post-modern Nero, without the facility for poetry. He is the new master of wrecking ball politics, the rich boy with an ego as big as the Ritz, who delights in busting things up to clear space for pleasure domes for the global elite. The broken lives left behind are just the cost of the deal. In this high stake game there's only one rule for survival: Find a scapegoat and move on.

— November 15, 2015

When Chivalry Fails

Did Hillary Clinton really win the diversionary spec-tacle known as the Iowa Caucuses by two-tenths of a percent? Probably not. But we will never know. Why? Because Bernie Sanders refuses to call the results into question and demand the release of the raw vote totals, which would likely show the senator won the actual vote by a decisive margin.

Sound familiar? It echoes Al Gore's "honorable" tactic during the 2000 recounts, when he refused to fight not only for his own elec-tion but also the voters (and members of the Congressional Black Caucus) who put it on the line for his campaign. As much as I like to credit Ralph Nader, Gore had only himself to blame for the debacle. Ditto: Bernie Sanders. Sanders had one real chance to derail Hillary Clinton: win Iowa and then New Hampshire. And he let it slip away.

The deflating outcome of the Iowa campaign must be a bitter dis-appointment to the young people flocking to his rallies, eager for a taste of real radical politics. I find Sanders's speeches rather dreary, the lugubrious moth-eaten rhetoric of a distant era. But you can't deny the continent-wide yearning for someone, anyone, who will attack the banks, Wall Street and the grinding economic inequality that is rupturing the republic. Those spirited Sandernistas are also rightly angered by the manifest corruption of a political system that treats them as outcasts.

The specious nature of the Iowa results only confirms those sus-picions, from coin flips to missing precinct workers to the notorious Microsoft vote-tabulating app (who would ever trust the company that created MS Windows?). Bernie should have been as furious as his band of collegiate san culottes. Instead, he raised the white flag of surrender. At that moment, the Clintons must have known they had his number. Panic averted.

Sanders seems to have learned how to campaign from reading Andreas Capellanus's *Art of Courtly Love*, the medieval code of chivalric conduct for romantic knights. Bernie could have taken a tutorial in how to confront the Clinton machine from Nader, but Sanders has stubbornly distanced himself by the most courageous populist political figure of our time. By contrast, the Clintons honed their political chops from Machiavelli and Charles Bronson movies. Even as shanks are being driven into his back, Sanders meekly refuses to frontally attack Clinton. He won't even deploy surrogates to blitz the Clintons on his behalf.

Yet the Clintons stand for everything Sanders claims to be against. They are the chief architects of the neoliberal takeover to the Democratic Party. They push austerity programs at home and abroad, while giving Wall Street traders the keys to the treasury. They slashed banking regulations and weakened environmental and food safety laws. They've rammed through job-killing trade pacts, from NAFTA to GATT and the WTO. They have supported interventionist wars from Kosovo to Colombia, Iraq to Libya. They gutted welfare, expanded the drug war and institutionalized the federal death penalty. All in the name of political realism. But Clintonian pragmatism only runs one direction: to the right. (See Diana Johnstone's *Queen of Chaos* for Hillary's full rap-sheet.)

Hillary knows Sander's pressure points. Any time Bernie even talks abstractly about her perfidious ties to Wall Street and Goldman Sachs, she emits a yelp of faux-outrage, charging "sexism" and demanding that Sanders apologize for "going negative." The Clintons must chuckle every night on their Snap Chat account about how easy it is to shame Sanders back into a posture of dutiful impotence. He's the dog that doesn't bite or even bark.

It's one thing to chivalrously declare that Hillary Clinton's email scandal is a manufactured controversy beneath debating. (It's not.) But it's something else entirely to let Hillary (who won Henry Kissinger's seal of approval) slither off the hook for the Libyan debacle itself, an intervention that Clinton seemingly had to force down Obama's throat. Libya is now the latest staging area for ISIS in North Africa. Of course, Sanders also supported the overthrow of Gaddafi and he's not one to apologize for his own mistakes.

Meanwhile, the Clintons are sharpening their campaign cutlery. These are the same people who deployed two staffers to Iowa in the heat of the 2008 campaign to publicly smear Barack Obama as a cocaine dealer. In fact, the entire premise of HRC's run against Obama was that America would never elect a black president and so, perhaps most notoriously in South Carolina, she and Bill played to racial prejudices within the party and the press. But Obama was made of sterner stuff and fought back aggressively, tagging Hillary again and again for her rancid vote to authorize the Iraq War. In revenge, Hillary drug out her doomed campaign until the last primary, refusing even then to concede. Why? Obama was squeaky clean. It seemed unlikely that a bimbo might erupt from one of his closets. Alexander Cockburn and I joked (with the creepy sensation that we just might have stumbled on to something) that Hillary was secretly hoping that Obama (who had been the target of more than 1,000 death threats) might be assassinated before the Democratic convention.

The Clinton hit teams are using the same playbook against Sanders. This time round the Clinton attack dogs are red-baiting Sanders, while seasoning the anti communist slurs with a sprinkling of southern anti-Semitism. Did you know, Bernie's a red? America will never elect a socialist. If he's nominated he'd bring the entire party down with him. There's even a whispering campaign now sweeping South Carolina about Sanders' religion. Did you know he was a *Jew*? Not only a Jew, but an atheist Jew? *A communist, atheist Jew!!* So it goes. What else would you expect from the Clinton's current political sicario, David Brock, the man who slimed Anita Hill?

In reality, the Sanders revolution was over before it started. The revolutionary aspiration expired the moment Sanders decided to run in the Democratic Party primaries, instead of as an independent, where he might have proved a real menace to the neoliberal establishment. Sanders even pledged to support HRC in the general election. What kind of "revolutionary" agrees to leave Marie Antoinette on the throne?

Revolutions aren't led by well-meaning wimps. Revolutions are about seizing power. They are about righting wrongs. Revolutions demand fierce confrontation and, as Robespierre might say, sharply-administered accountability. But Sanders was never interested in a real revolution. He's more Hubert Humphrey than Che Guevara—a timid reformer, an old-time liberal ranting in the antechambers of a party that has long since made its Faustian bargain with the agents of austerity. For the Democrats, there's no going back from that deal of shame.

Left and right, the sour mood of the country burns for a true political and economic rebellion. It may well happen. But look for it out on the streets, not in the hollow rituals of these elections.

— *February 5, 2016*

A Comedy of Terrors

POOR ISIS. TRY AS THEY MIGHT, THE MEN IN BLACK STILL CAN'T out-terrorize their enemies or, more pointedly, even their patrons. For the past three years, decapitations have served as the money shots for ISIS's theater of cruelty. Then on New Year's Day the Saudis upstaged ISIS by audaciously chopping off the heads of 47 men, including a prominent Shia cleric.

This act of brazen butchery is made all the more horrific by virtue of the fact that the Saudi head-slicers recently landed a seat on the UN Human Rights Council, largely at the insistence of Former British Prime Minister David Cameron, who personally vouched for the petro-autocracy's acute sensitivity to matters of civil liberties and the humane treatment of prisoners. Then again the drone-troika of Britain, France and the U.S. also enjoy seats on the council, so perhaps the Saudis have earned their slot after all.

With his peculiar fondness for porcine heads, Cameron was probably the Kingdom's most un-kosher ally, but he is far from Saudi Arabia's only political cheerleader. Showing a stunning lack of judgment, Comandante Bernie Sanders says his Syrian strategy relies on the Saudis taking the lead in the fight against ISIS. "They've got to get their hands dirty," Sanders inveighed to Wolf Blitzer on CNN. "They've got to get their troops on the ground. They've got to win that war with our support. We cannot be leading the effort."

Apparently Sanders skipped the briefing on how ISIS's apocalyptic ideology has been fueled by fire-breathing Wahhabi preachers financed by the Saudi royal family. The red senator also seems ignorant of the fact that ISIS functions as shock troops for the House of Saud in its proxy war against Iran, now raging in Yemen and Iraq, as well as Syria. You'd think that Bernie would be getting better advice from his friends in Israeli intelligence.

Sanders' policy on Syria is naïve to the point of doltishness. But Hillary's Syrian war plan—shared by most of her Republican rivals—borders on the pathological. Having not missed a minute of sleep haunted by the corpses of Libya, Mrs. Clinton is now stumping for the dismantling of Syria, using the carefully cultivated domestic anxiety over ISIS as the pretext. The cornerstone of Hillary's rogue scheme is the imposition of a no fly zone over that embattled country.

Sounds like a relatively benign plan, right? But wait. ISIS doesn't have an air force. They don't even a have drone. Russia, of course, *is* flying daily sorties in Syrian air space, at the invitation of the Syrian government, such as it is, and some kind of confrontation would be inevitable. Still, Hillary doesn't flinch. She has zealously vowed to shoot down *any* Russian plane that violated her unilateral ban.

Yet NATO's latest recruit, Turkey, jumped the gun. Recep Erdogan's trigger-happy generals didn't wait for any such fanciful legalisms and downed a Russian jet for momentarily breaching (perhaps) Turkish airspace. Then Turkamen fighters gleefully trained their machine-guns on the plane's pilots as they slowly parachuted toward the desert. Vladimir Putin fulminated boister-ously to his domestic audience, but prudently declined to retaliate against the Turks, perhaps intuiting that it would snap a tripwire for a full-frontal confrontation with NATO.

Everyone has been consulted about the future of Syria, except the Syrians themselves. Why? Because simply, Syrians don't matter. They are quite beside the point. Thanks to fresh reporting by Seymour Hersh, we now know that the subtext for Obama administration's Syrian strategy, dating back to Clinton's tenure at the State Department, has been largely geared toward ensnaring Russian in the Levantine quagmire. This is chaos theory marketed as foreign policy.

The rubble of modern Syria has become a multi-national bombing range, a kill zone of neo-Cold War contention. Each new act of domestic terrorism, from Paris to San Bernardino, has been used to rationalize more airstrikes on Syria, even though the killers in both slaughters seemed mainly to be attempting to impress the terror network, which is like blaming Jodie Foster for *inspiring* John Hinkley's wild fusillade at Reagan and his entourage.

Even Putin, that prickly hero to some precincts of the anti-imperialist Left, upped the ante by threatening to launch a nuclear strike against ISIS in response to the bombing of a Russian passenger plane over the Sinai, even though there's no direct evidence that the bomb was planted by the mad men of Daesh. Not to be outdone, Ted Cruz, the natural-born Canadian, vowed to make the sands of Raqqa glow, despite the fact that few Americans could point to Raqqa on a map or explain why this city of a quarter-million people should be incinerated in retribution for the murderous rampage by the Bonnie and Clyde of San Berdoo.

The war on terror has exploded in the face of the West, with spreading mayhem across the Middle East and unraveling conditions on the home front. One chilling measure of the savage toll from 14 years of war is the rate of military suicides in the US, which now total more than 1800 since the first cruise missiles struck Afghanistan. There is a desperate motive to externalize the blame for this bleak situation, to target a scapegoat. The rancid resumes of ISIS and the despotic Assad regime make Syria a convenient landscape for more imperial bloodletting. There's not even the faintest flicker of an anti-war movement left to impede their shameful enterprise.

In this comedy of terrors, the apex predators are the familiar ones circling overhead, waiting to blow Syria apart and plunder its bones.

— *February 12, 2016*

Blood Traces: Sanders and the Iraq War

Bernie Sanders has been shaming Hillary Clinton for her 2002 vote in support of George W. Bush's war against Saddam Hussein. Here Sanders is closely following Obama's 2008 playbook, where Obama used the Iraq war vote to repeatedly knock Clinton off balance.

But Sanders's shots at Clinton didn't inflict much damage this time around, largely because there's so little breathing space between the two candidates on foreign policy. Both Clinton and Sanders are seasoned interventionists, often advancing their hawkish policies under the ragged banner of "humanitarianism." (See: *Queen of Chaos* by Diana Johnstone.)

Sanders supported Bill Clinton's war on Serbia, voted for the 2001 Authorization Unilateral Military Force Against Terrorists (AUMF), which pretty much allowed Bush to wage war wherever he wanted, backed Obama's Libyan debacle and supports an expanded US role in the Syrian Civil War.

More problematic for the Senator in Birkenstocks is the little-known fact that Bernie Sanders himself voted *twice* in support of regime change in Iraq. In 1998 Sanders voted in favor of the Iraq Liberation Act of 1998, which said: "It should be the policy of the United States to support efforts to remove the regime headed by Saddam Hussein from power in Iraq and to promote the emergence of a democratic government to replace that regime."

Later that same year, Sanders also backed a resolution that stated: "Congress reaffirms that it should be the policy of the United States to support efforts to remove the regime headed by Saddam Hussein from power in Iraq and to promote the emergence of a democratic government to replace that regime." These measures gave congressional backing for the CIA's covert plan to overthrow the Hussein regime in Baghdad, as well as the tightening of an economic sanctions regime that may have killed as many as 500,000 Iraqi children. The resolution also gave the green light to Operation Desert Fox, a four-day long bombing campaign striking 100 targets throughout Iraq. The operation featured more than 300 bombing sorties and 350 ground-launched Tomahawk cruise missiles, several targeting Saddam Hussein himself.

Even Hillary belatedly admitted that her Iraq war vote was a mistake; Bernie, however, has never apologized for his two votes endorsing the overthrow of Saddam. On the rare occasions when Sanders has been confronted about these votes, he has casually dismissed them as being "almost unanimous." I went back and checked the record. In fact, many members of the progressive caucus in the House, as well as a few libertarian anti-war Members of Congress, voted against the Iraq regime change measures. Here's a list of the "no" votes on the Iraq Liberation Act of 1998:

Abercrombie	Bartlett
Brown (CA)	Carson
Chenoweth	Clay
Conyers	Davis (IL)
Doggett	Everett
Ewing	Ford
Furse	Hastings (FL)
Hilliard	Hostettler
Jackson (IL)	Jefferson
LaHood	Lee
Lewis (GA)	McKinney
Miller (CA)	Mink
Paul	Payne
Pombo	Rivers
Rush	Sabo
Serrano	Skaggs

Skelton	Stark
Towns	Vento
Walsh	Waters

So what changed? Only the party in power. In 1998, Bill Clinton was President, pursuing his own effort to takedown Saddam's government. In Clinton's State of the Union address of that year he laid the political groundwork for Bush's war:

"Saddam Hussein has spent the better part of this decade, and much of his nation's wealth, not on providing for the Iraqi people, but on developing nuclear, chemical and biological weapons and the missiles to deliver them. The United Nations weapons inspectors have done a truly remarkable job, finding and destroying more of Iraq's arsenal than was destroyed during the entire gulf war. Now, Saddam Hussein wants to stop them from completing their mission. I know I speak for everyone in this chamber, Republicans and Democrats, when I say to Saddam Hussein "You cannot defy the will of the world, and when I say to him, "You have used weapons of mass destruction before; we are determined to deny you the capacity to use them again."

Recall that over the 8 years of Clinton Time, Iraq was bombed an average of once every four days.

Even though Sanders markets himself as an "independent socialist," in fact, he has rarely dissented against the Democratic Party orthodoxy, especially when it comes to military intervention. That should permanently settle the notion of whether Bernie is a *real* Democrat. With the blood of 500,000 Iraqi children on his hands, surely Sanders has already won the "Humanitarian Warrior Seal of Approval," which leaves us with only one haunting question: Was it worth it, Senator Sanders?

— February 16, 2016

Bully on the Bench

THE MYTHOLOGIZING OF ANTONIN SCALIA BEGAN ONLY A FEW hours after his leathery heart stopped beating in West Texas and Satan swept his soul to the 8th Circle of the Inferno, where corrupt *barrators* are imprisoned for eternity. Here, strapped to a sparking electric chair, Scalia's torments will be supervised by the demon Malacoda, who, Dante informs us, regularly "makes a trumpet of his ass."

There was something of an uproar over the lack of an autopsy for Scalia's ravaged body. Quick-draw conspiracists alleged the portly associate justice was murdered to give Obama a chance to realign the Supreme Court. These creative thinkers seem not to have paid much attention to the bleak presence of Elena Kagan on the bench. There's no mystery about Scalia's death. A three pack a day man for most of his life, Scalia was clearly offed by his friends in the tobacco industry, whose murderous enterprise he zealously guarded in his legal opinions. And they say there's no justice.

It's not Scalia's corpse that needed dissecting, but the true nature and quality of his jurisprudence. From the *Weekly Standard* to the *Washington Post*, Scalia was lionized as a "titanic legal thinker," who possessed a blistering prose style and a wit "worthy of Swift." Even more bizarrely, the praise for Scalia's alleged brilliance was advanced by Beltway liberals, such as former Obama White House counsel Cass Sunstein (spouse of the odious Samantha Power) who asserted that Scalia was "witty, warm, funny and full of life. He was not only one of the most important justices in the nation's history; he was also one of the greatest." This curious assessment would have surprised former Chief Justice William Rehnquist, who for years sternly refused to assign any major court ruling to Scalia because he feared Scalia's mad legal theories and nasty prose style would undermine the standing of the court.

None of these attributes stand scrutiny. Any sober assessment of Scalia's legal writing would find them incoherent, contradictory and at times bordering on the pathological. In other words, he was a crank and bully, who was more than willing to consign a man to death row even when facts proved his innocence. In 2002, Scalia morbidly boasted about being part of "the machinery of death."

Over the years, Scalia constructed an image of himself as a crusty anachronism, a throwback to a pre-Lapsarian America, a kind of constitutional necromancer, who could divine meaning from a Constitution that he repeatedly claimed was "dead, dead, dead." But Scalia's concept of "originalism"—the view that the Constitution is constricted by the 18th century definitions of the language used by the Framers—is a less of a cogent legal theory than a shrewd smoke-screen. His crackpot legal theories served as legalistic camouflage for his own political prejudices and bigotry. Scalia often acted as if he, and he alone, could commune with the shade of James Madison to divine the original intent of a cohort of 18th century slave-owners on matters involving electronic wiretaps, drones and climate change.

Scalia's dissents lash out wildly at nearly every manifestation of modernity, from racial integration and affirmative action to abortion rights and environmental protection. These social advances Scalia viewed as part of the great antinomian threat to his starchy vision of the moral order of the universe. When it came to immigrant bashing, even Donald Trump would have to take a backseat to Scalia, who wrote in a 2013 dissent in the Arizona case that Americans feel "under siege by large numbers of illegal immigrants who invade their property, strain their social services, and even place their lives in jeopardy."

Nothing seemed to unnerve Scalia quite so much as his infantile revulsion at sodomy. He obsessively ranted about the "homosexual agenda," which threatened to infect the Republic and force god-fearing Americans to, as he put it in his risible dissent in *Lawrence v. Texas*, accept gays "as partners in their business, as scoutmasters for their children, as teachers at their children's schools, or as boarders in their houses."

Imagine being a bright young legal clerk having to research and draft these ludicrous and foul-minded opinions. By all accounts working for Scalia was a miserable exercise in career advancement. "He wasn't happy unless someone, somewhere, was suffering, preferably at his hands," said one of his former clerks, Bruce Hay, now a professor at Harvard Law School. "This was his jurisprudence."

Long rumored to be a member of the reactionary Opus Dei Catholic sect, Scalia wore his religion on his robes, even supervising Clarence Thomas's conversion to Catholicism. But Scalia was no mendicant. Indeed he was one of the most avaricious and gluttonous justices of the modern era. By 2014, Scalia had amassed a fortune of nearly $5 million, most of that sum accumulating after his elevation to the Court in 1986, through lavish speaking fees gleaned from conservative think tanks and corporate chieftains, some of whom had cases pending before the court.

Scalia expired in his barbarous element: alone in bed, breathing mask on his nightstand, at a swank resort, after a day of blood sport sponsored by a creepy cult of millionaire hunters called the Order of St. Hubertus, as coyotes chuckled in the distance. Play on, Malacoda.

— *February 20, 2016*

Hand Jobs: Heidegger, Hitler and Trump

MARCO RUBIO WAS THE FIRST TO WARN US. IN MARCH, LITTLE Marco admonished all Americans to scrutinize Trump's hands before giving him their vote, hands which Rubio rather giddily alleged served as a signifier of the tycoon's secret short-comings.

So look closely at those mitts and digits: the short, rather stubby fingers, the neatly polished nails, the fleshy palms, all immaculately bronzed, as if dipped in a fine shellac.

What are we to make of them? Is there a political precedent for such wonderfully manicured but physically diminutive political paws?

For purposes of edification, let us consult a little known encounter between two of the 20th century's most consequential philosophers, one celebrated, one infamous.

The setting is Germany. The year is 1933. The scene is the Heidelberg house of Karl Jaspers and his Jewish wife and collaborator Gertrude. A guest is coming for dinner, an old friend and fellow phenomenologist who had just been appointed rector of Freiburg University. The meal is meant to be a celebration of their friend's lofty new post.

The guest is, of course, none other than Martin Heidegger, author of the opaquely written but massively influential *Being and Time*. What Karl and Gertrude Jaspers don't know, but will soon discover to their disbelief, is that their friend and intellectual sparring partner has just joined the National Socialist Germany Workers Party and arrives at their doorstep wearing a shiny Nazi pin on his lapel.

A debate between the two big brains soon erupts over a meal of Sauerbraten and potato dumplings. When Jaspers assails Heidegger's pact with the Nazis, Heidegger waves his hand dismissively and ominously advises Karl and Gertrude that it is now time for "one to step in line."

Jaspers counters: "But my dear friend, you can't possibly mean that. It's like 1914 all over again. The deceitful mass intoxication! What about the pursuit of knowledge, which the Nazis demean? What about education, which Hitler lacks and thus reviles?"

Heidegger cuts Jaspers off abruptly. "Education is irrelevant," the moral philosopher of Nazism shouts. "Just look at his wonderful hands!"

Moral: the smaller the hands, the more fanatic the compensation.

Cautionary note: You might want to size up Hillary's diminutive hands before you cast that fatal ballot.

— *March 15, 2016*

The Candidate Who Came in From the Cold

> "In the end, glorification of splendid underdogs is nothing other than the glorification of the splendid system that makes them so."
> —Theodor Adorno

BERNIE SANDERS LOST THE MOMENT HE BECAME ENTRANCED BY the prospect that he might win. What did he lose? His grip on political reality.

For most of his life Sanders has cultivated the role of political cynic, a professional outsider, a grand-standing critic of The System. Once he came in from the cold and converted from independent socialist to a Democrat (for life, according to his campaign manager Jeff Weaver) that hard-boiled cynicism—one's tempted to call it realism—eroded away in the face of large crowds of adoring supporters, from Portland, Maine to Portland, Oregon. Is it possible that Sanders became intoxicated by the floridness of his own rhetoric?

The results from the New York primary perfectly distill the promise and the heartbreak of Sanders's Quixotic campaign for the Democratic Party nomination. Coming off of his thrashing of Hillary Clinton in Wisconsin, Sanders enjoyed all of the momentum, media attention and energy heading toward the big stakes in New York. Even so, there was no chance that he could win the Empire State. The rules were against him, the demographics were against him, the System was against him. The polls showed him down by more than 10 points and barely twitched in the two weeks after Wisconsin. Yet a few days before the primary, Sanders confidently predicted victory. It was not a rational statement.

In the end, Hillary won New York by almost exactly the same margin that she defeated Barack Obama by 2008. Sanders might take some solace in the fact that he actually performed fractionally better than Obama. But he shouldn't. In 2008, Obama, despite his loss in New York, was on his way to the Democratic nomination. Sanders, by contrast, is going nowhere at all, except in registering tens of thousands of new young voters as Democrats.

Welcome to the machine, kids.

Of course, each time Bernie loses, under circumstances where the DNC establishment has fragrantly conspired against him, the senator raises freshets of more money online (at $27 a pop), thus encouraging him to continue his doomed crusade. Yet this steady stream of cash functions as a kind of fool's gold. Bernie actually outspent Hillary in New York and the spending did him almost no good.

I'm no fan of the Senator from Ben and Jerry's, but, as the founding member of ABHoR (Anybody But Hillary Rodham), I stubbornly clung to my own fantasies about Sanders. Naively, I believed that if Bernie had fought to have the Iowa votes released, challenged the curious results in Nevada and Missouri and attacked the Super Delegate system he could have found a foothold, exposing how the DNC had rigged the process for Hillary. But that was delusional. In fact, there was almost certainly no pathway to victory for Sanders in the Democratic primaries. Perversely, Sanders's team spent their last gasp courting the anti-democratic Super Delegates in an attempt to neutralize Hillary's insurmountable lead in awarded delegates. Why? More than 90 percent of Super Delegates had already pledged their votes to Clinton. Aside from her indictment, what could possibly induce them to change their minds and back someone who, until a few months ago, wasn't even a member of their party? In any event, groveling for Super Delegates must surely be seen as the final humiliation of the Sanders campaign, a calculated political betrayal of everything the campaign claimed to be about.

So Bernie was bound to lose. He knew it. His staff knew it. Only his loyal claque of Sandernistas seem to have been kept in the dark regarding the inevitable outcome. Bernie owed it to his supporters to tell them the truth about the rigged nature of the primaries, instead of injecting them with the rhetoric of false hope. In the absence of that dose of political reality, Sanders's supporters began looking for scapegoats to explain the inexplicable losses of their hero against an unappetizing and deeply compromised opponent. Most frequently, the distraught Sandernistas have focused their rage on black voters. Apparently, many Sandernistas subscribe to the Charles "Bell Curve" Murray school of political science. They seem to believe that African-Americans are so intellectually limited that they don't know what's good for them. I suspect the next thing will be for the Sandernistas to propose having enlightened white progressives cast proxy votes on behalf of blacks. Bernie himself continues to fuel this toxic scenario, most recently when he decried the frontloading of southern primaries, which are dominated by black voters. The Sanders campaign's slurs against American blacks are uglier than anything they've launched at Hillary Clinton.

What Sanders and his Sandernistas could have done was to take the rotten hulk of the Democratic Party down with them. But that was never in the cards. Why? For starters, many of Sanders's top advisers, such as Tad Davine, are Democratic Party loyalists, who will certainly want jobs in other Democratic campaigns in the next election cycle. More pressingly, although Bernie talks of political revolution, he's a reformer not a radical. His goal is to refashion the Democratic Party from the inside. In this respect, Sanders is an old-fashioned liberal, not a revolutionary socialist. No surprise there. His entire political life testifies to his liberal incrementalism. The man has been in elected office since 1981, tweaking at the gears instead of monkey-wrenching the machine. If Sanders now seems like a radical, it's only a measure how far to the right the Democrats have migrated since the rise of the neoliberals. Sanders may be as good as a Democrat gets (aside from Barbara Lee), but how good is that? And what will it get you? Single payer health care? Nationalization of the banks? Abolition of nuclear weapons? Dream on.

More and more this vaunted "movement" seems to be little more than a kind of moveable feast, which follows Sanders around like a swarm of post-modern Deadheads, from venue to venue, to hear the senator deliver the same tepid stump speech he's been warbling for the last 8 months. In the end, Bernie Sanders proved to be an unconventional candidate running a fairly conventional campaign, in the Dean 2004/Obama 2008 mold. This gives rise to the suspicion that the Sanders Movement is mostly about the glorification of one Bernard Sanders.

What might a real movement have done? If Sanders could turn 30,000 people out for a pep rally in Washington Square Park, why couldn't he have had a flash mob demonstration mustering half that many fervent supporters to shut down Goldman Sachs for a day? If he could lure 20,000 Hipsters to the Rose Garden in Portland, why couldn't he turn out 10,000 Sandernistas to bolster the picket lines of striking Verizon workers? If Sanders could draw 15,000 people in Austin, Texas, why couldn't his movement bring 5,000 people to Huntsville to protest executions at the Texas death house? If Sanders could draw 18,000 people to a rally in Las Vegas, why couldn't he just as easily have led them in a protest at nearby Creech Air Force Base, the center of operations for US predator drones? Strike that. Sanders supports Obama's killer drone program. My bad. But you get the point. Instead of being used as stage props, why hasn't Sanders put his teaming crowds of eager Sandernistas to work doing the things that *real* movements do: blocking the sale of a foreclosed house in Baltimore, disrupting a fracking site in rural Pennsylvania, shutting down the entrance to the police torture chamber at Homan Square in Chicago for a day, intervening between San Diego cops and the homeless camp they seek to evict? Why? Because that's not who Bernie Sanders is and that's not what his movement is about. He's willing to rock the neoliberal boat, but not sink it.

Ultimately, Bernie Sanders is a loyalist to liberalism. That's why he voted for Bill Clinton's racist Crime Bill. It's why he voted twice to overthrow Saddam Hussein during Clinton time and endorsed a cruel sanctions regime that killed more than 400,000 innocent Iraqi kids. It's why he backed the Clinton war on Serbia, voted for the AUMF that has been used to justify total and enduring war since

9/11, backed the Libyan intervention and, most crucially, pledged to support Hillary. So let's dispense with this year of magical thinking and get back to work in the real war against neoliberalism in all its guises. Take a cue from Bob Marley, Senator, and tell the children the truth: every vote for Sanders was a vote for Clinton.

— *April 22, 2016*

Good as Goldman

NOTHING SEEMS TO RATTLE HILLARY CLINTON QUITE SO MUCH AS pointed questions about her personal finances. How much she's made. How she made it. Where it all came from. From her miraculous adventures in the cattle futures market to the Whitewater real estate scam, many of the most venal Clinton scandals down the decades have involved Hillary's financial entanglements and the serpentine measures she has taken to conceal them from public scrutiny.

Hillary is both driven to acquire money and emits a faint whiff of guilt about having hoarded so much of it. One might be tempted to ascribe her squeamishness about wealth to her rigid Methodism, but her friends say that Hillary's covetousness derives from a deep obsession with feeling secure, which makes a kind of sense given Bill's free-wheeling proclivities. She's not, after all, a child of the Depression, but a baby boomer. Hillary was raised in comfortable circumstances in the Chicago suburbs and, unlike her husband, has never in her life felt the sting of want.

Mrs. Clinton's stubborn refusal to disclose the text of her three speeches to Goldman Sachs executives in the fall of 2013 fits this self-destructive pattern of greed and guilt. She was fortunate that Bernie Sanders proved too feeble a candidate to seize the advantage. Each time Sanders was asked to show a nexus between the $675,000 she was paid and any political favors to the financial vultures at Goldman, the senator froze, proving strangely incapable of driving a stake into the heart of her campaign.

A less paranoid politician would have simply released the tedious transcripts of the speeches on a Friday evening to bore insomniac readers to sleep. The real question, of course, was never about the content of the speeches, but about why Goldman was paying her $225,000 an hour to give them. Goldman executives weren't huddling around Mrs. Clinton to listen to her recite the obscurantist mish-mash ghost-dictated by her top economic advisor Alan Blinder. Blinder, a well-known Wall Street commodity himself, is a former vice-chair of the Federal Reserve and co-founder of Promontory Interfinancial Network, a regulatory arbitrage outfit whose top executives pocket $30 million a year. Blinder has publicly assured his Wall Street pals that Clinton will not under any circumstances break up the big banks and neither will she seek to reanimate Glass-Steagall, the Depression-era regulatory measure whose exsanguination by her husband enabled the financial looting by firms like Goldman and Lehman Brothers that spurred the global economic collapse of 2008.

The lavish fee from Goldman for Hillary's speeches was both a gratuity for past loyalty and a down payment on future services. Goldman's ties to the Clintons date back at least to 1985, when Goldman executives began pumping money into the newly formed Democratic Leadership Council, a kind of proto-SuperPac for the advancement of neoliberalism. Behind its "third-way" politics smokescreen, the DLC was shaking down corporations and Wall Street financiers to fund the campaigns of business-friendly "New" Democrats such as Al Gore and Bill Clinton.

The DLC served as the political launching pad for the Clintons, boosting them out of the obscurity of the Arkansas dog-patch into the rarified orbit of the Georgetown cocktail circuit and the Wall Street money movers. By the time Bill rambled through his interminable keynote speech at the 1988 Democratic Convention, the Clintons' Faustian pact with Goldman had already been inked, their political souls cleansed of any vestiges of the southern populism Clinton had exploited so effortlessly during his first term as governor.

In 1991, the Clintons traveled to Manhattan, where they tested the waters for Bill's then rather improbable presidential bid. At a dinner meeting with Goldman's co-chair Robert Rubin, Clinton made his case as a more pliant political vessel than George H.W. Bush, who many of the younger Wall Street raiders had soured on. Rubin emerged from the dinner so impressed that he agreed to serve as one of the campaign's top economic advisors. More crucially, Rubin soon began orchestrating a riptide of Wall Street money into Clinton's campaign war chest, not only from Goldman but also from other banking and investment titans, such as Lehman Brothers and Citibank, who were eager to see the loosening of federal financial regulations. With Rubin priming the pump, Clinton's campaign coffers soon dwarfed his rivals and enabled him to survive the sex scandals that detonated on the eve of the New Hampshire primary.

After his election, Clinton swiftly returned the favor checking off one item after another on Rubin's wish list, often at the expense of the few morsels he'd tossed to the progressive base of the party. In a rare fit of pique, Clinton erupted during one meeting of his National Economic Council, which Rubin chaired, in the first fraught year of his presidency by yelling: "You mean my entire agenda has been turned over to the fucking bond market?" Surely, Bill meant this as a rhetorical question.

When the time came to do the serious business of deregulating the financial sector, Rubin migrated from the shadows of the NEC to become Treasury Secretary, where he oversaw the implementation of NAFTA, the immiseration of the Mexican economy, imposed shock therapy on the struggling Russian economy, blocked the regulation of credit derivatives and gutted Glass-Steagall. When Rubin left the Treasury to cash in on his work at Citigroup, Clinton called him "the greatest secretary of the Treasury since Alexander Hamilton." Nine years later, following the greatest upward transfer of wealth in history, the global economy was in ruins, with Clinton, Rubin and Goldman Sachs' fingerprints all over the carnage.

In mid-May, Hillary announced her intention to make Bill the "economic czar" for her administration. This served to quell any anxiety that she might have been infected during the primary campaign by the Sanders virus. For Wall Street, the Clintons are still as good as Goldman. *Quid pro quo.*

— May 22, 2016

The Once and Future Sandernistas

It ended the way it began, with Bernie Sanders drawing huge energetic crowds and winning few votes from blacks and Hispanics. Sanders could never connect with the most vulnerable voters in the country. That fact alone doomed his campaign.

Those vast crowds seemed to have acted on Sanders like a kind of opiate, numbing him to the political reality of his campaign. As noted in a recent *Politico* article, the Sanders campaign staff had known for months that the senator had no path to victory. Instead of being honest with their supporters, the Sanders campaign fed them one illusory scenario after another. Even Sanders himself got seduced by the fairy tale.

There's no loyalty anymore. In that same *Politco* article, Sanders's top political hired-hacks took pleasure in plunging anonymous knives into their leader's back, blaming him for every misstep in the campaign. These professional turncoats are simply trying to scrub any lingering stains off their own hands and polish up their resumés for a job with Team Clinton. On the other hand, Bernie hired these deplorable operatives. You get what you pay for.

The dream campaign came to an abrupt end with Sanders's crushing defeat in California. Bernie camped out in the Golden State for two weeks, doing three or four large events a day. The senator seemed energized by the sunshine and the adoring crowds. He was transfixed by his own hype.

But Sanders never had any real chance to win California. The demographics and party establishment were aligned against him. California is a machine state and Sanders didn't throw enough monkeywrenches into the gears. In the end, he lost by more than 400,000 votes, a humiliating margin that can't be written off to voter suppression or hacked machines. Such conspiracy mongering only serves to deflect attention from the real defects that fatally crippled the

Sanders campaign. The stakes are too high to surrender to magical thinking.

Running as an economic revolutionary, Sanders spent most of his time in the cozy milieu of college campuses instead of in desolate urban landscapes or working-class suburbs. It's hard to earn the trust of poor people when you don't spend much time in their company.

Many inconsolable Sandernistas continue to reflexively blame blacks and Hispanics for backing Clinton, whose odious policies offer only a few morsels to temper the grinding misery of poor people. But Sanders didn't do much to endear himself to the American underclass.

Sanders chided Clinton for her vote on the Iraq War, saying it disqualified her from being president. Yet, he never satisfactorily explained his own vote for the Clinton Crime Bill, which launched a 20-year long war on America's blacks and Hispanics. If blacks voting for Clinton seemed irrational, blacks could easily justify a vote against Sanders for his role in backing the racially-motivated incarceration of millions of black Americans and putting 100,000 new cops onto the streets of urban America, with the predictable results: ruined lives and dead youths. Payback is a bitch.

Of course, Sanders could have turned his anemic appeal to black Democratic voters to his advantage. It might have liberated him to frontally attack Obama's dismal record (instead of huddling with him at the White House) as well as Hillary's, without fear of losing support he never had.

His curious timidity against confronting Obama's policies, from drone warfare to the president's bailout of the insurance industry (AKA ObamaCare), hobbled Sanders from the starting gate. Obama and Hillary Clinton are both neoliberals, who have betrayed organized labor and pushed job-killing trade pacts across the world. Both are beholden to the energy cartels, backing widespread oil drilling, fracking and nuclear power. Both are military interventionists, pursuing wars on at least 12 different fronts, from Afghanistan to Yemen. Of course, Hillary and Obama are simply manifestations of the power structure of the Democratic Party itself, which is unapologetically hawkish. The same party Sanders belatedly joined.

But Sanders proved singularly incapable of targeting the imperialist ideology of the Obama/Clinton era. In fact, the senator is visibly uncomfortable when forced to talk about foreign policy. Even after the assassination of Goldman Prize winner Berta Cáceres by thugs associated with the Honduran regime, Sanders inexplicably refused to press Clinton on her backing of the Honduran coup that put Cácere's killers into power. Similarly, Sanders awkwardly failed to land any punches against Hillary for her catastrophic Libyan debacle.

Sanders himself has blamed the Democratic Party for his loss, charging that the primary process was rigged by super-delegates, purged voter rolls, hackable voting machines and the pro-Clinton machinations of Debbie (Does DNC) Wasserman-Schultz. This is the silliest excuse of all. This may come as a shock, but the Democratic Party is not a democratic institution. The function of the party is to promote politicians who adhere to the ideology of the party, which has been sternly neoliberal since the nomination of Jimmy Carter in 1976. To the extent that the party machine suppressed the Sanders insurgency, it wasn't a matter of corruption but self-preservation.

But for most of the last 10 months, Sanders wasn't treated too harshly by the party. He certainly wasn't "McGoverned" by the party's political black bag teams and dirty tricksters. In fact, the Democrats were surely gratified to see Sanders out there, drawing attention to a dull and lifeless party that would otherwise have been totally eclipsed by the Trump media blitzkrieg. Sanders served the valuable function of energizing and registering on the Democratic Party rolls tens of thousands of new voters, who otherwise would have been content to stay at home playing Warcraft and Snapchatting about the latest Kardashian outrage. And the party elites knew from the beginning that he never had even an outside chance at beating

Hillary. The race was over after Super Tuesday, when Hillary swept the southland. The rest has been political theater.

The biggest threat that Sanders posed to the Democratic machine was his ability to raise independent money, and lots of it, outside of the party's control. The most recent tally shows that Sanders raised more than $212 million, a staggering amount, mostly from small online donors. He didn't incur large debts and doesn't owe any financial obligations to the usual Democratic Party loan sharks. He broke the money-dispensing monopoly of the DNC and deserves credit for that.

But where did all of that money go? Most of it went to those duplicitous consultants. Bernie raised money quickly, but his campaign had a high "bern" rate and there's precious little left to show for squandering all those millions. Imagine the havoc Black Lives Matter could unleash with only half of that warchest.

Sanders built a *"yuuge"* following. It's yet to be determined whether these youthful hordes can be mobilized into a real movement. The movement is certainly going nowhere as long as Sanders loyalists remain locked inside the entropic hothouse of the Democratic Party, where their hero has led and left them, awaiting a couple of planks in the platform drafted in disappearing ink.

The most energetic political movement in the country right now is the combative Chicano-led masses stalking Trump and his racist retinue from venue-to-venue. If only there existed a similar movement haunting Hillary's every step.

Real political revolutions (as opposed to rhetorical ones) begin after the futility of the ballot box has been proven. Sustainable movements are driven by issues not personalities. And sometimes you have to bust your idols for kindling to get things ignited.

Your move, Sandernistas.

— June 10, 2016

A PUBLIC BERNING
IMPROVISED NOTES FROM THE
DEMOCRATIC CONVENTION

Day One: Don't Cry for Me DNC

By the time the Democratic Convention came along in late July, no one at CounterPunch *was willing to cover the damn thing, even via the Tube. Deva had absconded to float the Klamath River. Conveniently, Nathaniel had neglected to pay his cable bill for three months. Becky was busy midwifing the births of baby goats. And Joshua had snuck off in search of six-inch waves to surf at Bolsa Chica. So it was left to me to enter the virtual combat zone solo, armed only with my Macintosh, three bottles of El Buho Mezcal and a fanny-pack of edibles infused with Oregon's newly legalized agricultural product. What follows are my "instantaneous impressions" of those strange four days, written moment-by-moment as the convention unfolded in hour after hour of surreal tedium. In the end, the whole show held a sick attraction, like watching a slow running snuff film of a political revolution, as a malign darkness descended on the Republic.*

¶ DEBBIE WASSERMAN SCHULTZ WAS AWFUL AT EVERYTHING SHE did except ensuring HRC's nomination. This was not lost on her own delegation in Florida, who shouted her down when she attempted to speak on the morning of July 25. Two hours later she had been removed from her position as chair of the DNC, banned from the stage at the convention and rewarded with an obscure position with the Clinton campaign. After Debbie loses her primary contest to Tim Canova, she'll land some kind of position with the Clinton administration. So...

> Don't cry for me, DNC!
> I've still got my jewelry
> and part of an oil refinery...
> Hillary's going make me an Ambassador
> and not to some shithole like El Salvador.
> I'm thinking Luxembourg or Monaco

Where I'll be driven around in a pink El Dorado…

Failing that, there's always the Ambassador to Nordstrom's.

⁋ According to MS-DNC, the whole story of the DNC email dump that exposed how Party elites tried to rig the primary elections for HRC is really about how Putin and his hackers are trying to fix the fall election for Trump. How bad do Democrats hate WikiLeaks and Julian Assange? Well, here's Democratic fixer Bob Beckel on Assange: "The guy ought to be and I'm not for the death penalty, so if I'm not for the death penalty, there's only one way to do it: illegally shoot the son of a bitch."

⁋ Remarkable! Bernie Sanders is getting shouted down by his own delegates this morning for pushing Hillary & Kaine down their throats.

If the double blows of the DNC email dump and the Kaine pick didn't push Bernie over the brink, nothing will. He made his Faustian pact and now he is just another Clinton surrogate.

⁋ Misogyny, Liberal-style: I think it's unfair that Debbie Wasserman Schultz is taking all the heat for the DNC email scandal. After all, Obama is the real leader of the DNC. Debbie is Obama's hand-picked proxy. Obama should follow Debbie's lead and cancel his speech tomorrow night. It's only proper.

⁋ According to a report in the *New York Times*, the "LOCK HER UP! LOCK HER UP!!" chant has spread to Philly: "The reaction from Mr. Sanders's supporters was consistent with the anti-Clinton message delivered by demonstrators earlier in the day. Some pro-Sanders protesters took a harder turn on Monday, chanting 'Lock her up' in an echo of the message of the Republican National Convention a week earlier, fueled by the resignation of the chairwoman of the Democratic National Committee."

⁋ After a supposedly disastrous, widely-ridiculed convention, Trump was now up 5%. He might well be up 10 after the Democrats finish theirs… They continue to ignore working class issues and the rising public animus toward interventionist wars at their peril. The fact that all this seems inexplicable to them will help seal their fate.

❡ According to CNN,

"'Trump's new edge rests largely on increased support among independents, 43% of whom said that Trump's convention in Cleveland left them more likely to back him, while 41% were dissuaded. Pre-convention, independents split 34% Clinton to 31% Trump, with sizable numbers behind Johnson (22%) and Stein (10%). Now, 46% say they back Trump, 28% Clinton, 15% Johnson and 4% Stein."

Note that MS-DNC is reporting only a 3% Trump lead, because they stubbornly ignore the presence of Gary Johnson and Jill Stein. But both of the third party candidates are drawing more votes from Clinton than from Trump.

❡ Nancy Pelosi was booed as she addressed her own California delegation. Who wants to be the next Democratic power broker to step up to the microphone? Chuck Schumer, stop hiding behind the curtains, you've never been shy before!

Michael Yates sent me this note: "Pelosi is a real slimeball. No doubt Sanders will have good things to say about her."

❡ Benediction booed. Barney Frank booed. Marcia Fudge booed. Next? This convention could be fun, after all!

❡ After waiting three days to apologize to Sanders and the Sandernistas for rigging the democratic process against his campaign, Democratic leaders now urge Sandernistas to be "respectful" of the "democratic process"!

❡ Sanders in Full Clinton Mode, just texted his delegates to sit back and take it in silence: "I ask you as a personal courtesy to me to not engage in any kind of protest on the floor."

Imagine what the scene on the floor would be like had Sanders *not* endorsed HRC. What a monumental failure of nerve on his part.

❡ Will the Sandernistas have to stop calling themselves Sandernistas?

¶ Sanders: "Friends, settle down! Settle down! When I said 'revolution' I didn't mean a cap-R 'Revolution. It was a METAPHOR!'"

¶ How badly the Clintons misread the mood of their own rapidly-dwindling base when they picked the pro-TPP Kaine, after knowing that the DNC's emails had been released. There's stupidity. And there's hubris. Hillary's got massive quantities of both.

The TPP bait-and-switch is crucial here because it exposes that Hillary lied about her own position and thus confirms everyone's belief in her mendacity.

¶ Hillary seems to have spent more time courting Michael Bloomberg than the Steelworkers.

¶ The DNC, with the help of the hired Sanders flacks, just pushed through the platform on a voice vote, steamrolling efforts by the Sandernistas and Labor to get a floor vote on the TPP.

¶ Hillary delegates are holding up signs reading "Love Trumps Hate." Can't that be read in two entirely different ways?

¶ The Democratic Convention is highlighting the drug war. Not eliminating it, mind you, but extending it to the so-called "opioid epidemic." Will they call for ending the Afghan War which has accelerated the poppy trade? Will they go after prescription-pushing Big Pharma, coddled so tenderly by Tim Kaine? Dream on, Dems. Where's Tipper Gore?

Rules of Engagement for HRC's Drug War: If you take your opioids in pill form (i.e., white people) you go to therapy. If you use a needle (i.e., blacks and Hispanics), you go to prison. Shoot them only if you see them shooting up.

¶ Fascinating interview with Julian Assange on NBC about the DNC email dump. Assange said the Russian hack of the DNC computers occurred before many of the emails in this document dump were even written. He said that the DNC's email system was almost transparent. The system had very little security and that the emails were there for the taking. He said the RNC system is equally vulnerable. (Look out Reince Priebus!)

What a triumph for Assange and WikiLeaks. The fact that the CIA hasn't been able to eliminate WikiLeaks is a real & tangible sign of hope. You can bet they'll be near the top of Hillary's hit list if she's elected.

¶ Does Sen. Kirsten Gillibrand not know that after college Hillary DID in fact go to work for "a fancy law firm," called Rose Law, where she toiled, not on behalf of "the children", but for some of the South's most vicious corporations and did a good enough job that she was invited to join the board of Wal-Mart?

¶ Listening to Clinton's campaign guru Robby Mook mewl about possible Russian meddling in US elections is like listening to Trump whine about income tax rates when he apparently pays nothing. Shall we recall HRC's direct intervention in the Russian elections? Her financing of the opposition in the Venezuelan elections? Her role in the Honduran coup? That's essentially the job description of the Secretary of State, isn't it? What goes around comes around, Hillary. (If it proves, in fact, to be the case that the hackers were Russians.)

¶ It's 9 PM in Philly and all is quiet on the eastern front. Has the steam gone out of the Sandernistas? After a raucous morning, I hope they didn't spend the afternoon sharing bong hits of DNC Trainwreck or Burlington Kush. Did they all mellow out? Popping a few Bernie Bennies would have been a better choice....

¶ Sarah "Sandernista" Silverman just slammed Sandernistas as being "ridiculous." Make her a diplomat in the Clinton State Dept. We'll be going to war with Grenada again before you know it....

¶ Enough with dreary Paul "Way Back Machine" Simon. Bring back, Demi "I Have a Mental Illness" Lovato!

❡ Cory Booker has none of the oratorical gifts of Obama. He's more of a second rate blues shouter than a true master of political soul.

❡ Did Booker flub the line about Hillary "paying it forward" her entire life? Surely he meant she's been "getting paid" forward her entire life?

❡ Booker: "Hillary doesn't believe in scapegoating people over their religion." Did Mrs. Clinton come to this position after or before she fired Debbie Wasserman Schultz for plotting to scapegoat Sanders over his religion?

❡ Look, there's Bill Clinton lustily applauding Michelle Obama. Recall when he slandered her husband's campaign for race-baiting: "I think that they played the race card on me. We now know, from memos from the campaign, that they planned to do it all along." And, unforgettably, telling Joe Biden: "A few years ago, this guy would have been carrying our bags."

❡ Michelle's got the gift. She understands, as McLuhan said decades ago, that TV is a cool medium. She's the coolest thing they've got going. Too bad she's squandering it on someone who led her husband into the Libyan debacle.

❡ Once again, Michelle invokes HRC's tome *It Takes a Village*. But as Secretary of State, Hillary's playbook was "To Drone a Village". My friend Carl Estabrook (*il miglior fabbro*) amended this to: "To Take Out a Village".

❡ Michelle's going to get shit tomorrow for saying she "wakes up every morning in a house built by slaves."

❡ Pretty low-wattage speech from Warren. Probably a bad move to put her after Michelle. The Bernie or Bust block has thrown off her rhythm a few times, with the Sandernistas screaming: "We trusted you!" Her heart doesn't seem to be in her blurbs for HRC and Kaine.

❡ Biggest applause line for Warren came when she quoted Trump's line about the "system being rigged." But the crowd seemed placid and unimpressed. Warren's encomiums for Hillary on economic justice and trade fell flat, with the crowd chanting "Goldman Sachs! Goldman Sachs!"

❡ Sandernistas crying as Bernie takes the stage. Too bad it's not the Clintons crying. If only Picasso were around to paint Bernie's weeping women…What a strange magnetism he has, especially his appeal to younger women, who were the backbone of his campaign. Is it a longing for the lost grandfather? The appeal is almost mystical. Patrick Flaherty suggested that it was "a longing for a sincere, strong, open-hearted male, which is all too rare in popular culture." But look where he led them: right into the arms of the Wicked Stepmother.

❡ The boos began the moment Bernie began his refrain: "Hillary understands…"

❡ Bernie's vouching for Hillary, the Secretary of Fracking, on climate change rang pretty hollow, especially when she doubled-down with Tim "Offshore Drilling" Kaine. What's worse? Someone who dismisses the science and supports the oil, gas and coal industry or someone, like Clinton and Kaine, who understands the science and still gives the fossil fuel lobby all they want?

❡ Sanders is no Jesse Jackson in the rhetoric dept. Although with both of them you end up in the same place. Back where you started. Bernie sounded like a political prisoner reciting lines written by James Carville. A willing prisoner.

❡ Bernie kept repeating the withered platitude that "We're stronger when we stand together." But together with whom? For what? Perhaps all the tears were for the ragged spectacle of Sanders humiliating himself for 50 straight minutes on behalf of a ticket which has only contempt for him and his followers.

¶ *The New York Times* headline on Sanders' political role at the Convention pretty much said it all: "Leader of a Revolt Now Must Put One Down." Poor Bernie: he started out as Danton and ends up as Edmund Burke.

¶ Mike Whitney sends me a note from the backwoods of northwest Washington State: "As has happened so often before, the Democratic Party has become the graveyard of a movement of social protest, with Sanders serving as the undertaker."

¶ All in all, it was a fun yet exhausting experiment in trying to annotate an entire day at the Democratic convention. I have a new respect for obsessive Tweeters like Doug Henwood. It reminded me of how different things are now from 2000, when I was the "color commentator" for BBC Radio on the final night of the Democratic Convention in Los Angeles and the BBC announcer kept trying to get me to say that Al Gore had suddenly found a new spark of energy. I replied to his displeasure, "Yes, like the Mummy after his reanimation." That was the night Al tongue raped Tipper Gore in front of an international TV audience. I doubt Hillary will tongue rape Bill on Thursday night. But we can always hope. To paraphrase Alexander Cockburn on the Soviet invasion of Afghanistan, if anyone ever deserved to be raped on live TV it's Bill Clinton…

Day Two: The Humiliation Games

❡ THE BIG NEWS OF THE MORNING WAS THE VINDICATION OF A ground-breaking story that Margaret Kidder wrote for *CounterPunch* earlier in 2016. Buried inside the 20,000 DNC emails released by WikiLeaks were documents confirming a tricky financial scam orchestrated by the DNC and the Clinton campaign, whereby money that was meant for state Democratic parties was re-routed to the Clinton machine in order to evade campaign finance laws, thus making a mockery of Hillary's recent pledge to get the Big Money out of politics. We published Kidder's explosive piece on the first of April and it spread like lightning across the Net. Within a few days, her exposé had been read by more than one million people and had received more than 50,000 Facebook shares (whatever that means). The Clinton machine shifted into attack mode, their default position. Clinton trolls first started rumors that the story was an April Fools' Day prank. When that attack floundered, the Clinton slime operation set their sights on the author herself. The article was written by Margot Kidder, *the actress*, they said with misogynistic condescension. You know, Lois Lane. You can't trust her. She's had mental health issues. So much for feminism... This kind of viciousness is standard operating procedure in Clintonworld. But how wrong they were. Margot Kidder is one of the smartest people I know. She's very well read, is a determined researcher and writes with clarity and force. She's also fearless. Margot had the goods on them and now there's no doubt. Heroic work, Margot!

❡ The Democrats are working overtime to transform the DNC email episode into a story about Russian hackers, Putin and Trump. One Democratic Party flack called it the most outrageous political break-in since Watergate. Anything to divert attention from the scandalous content of the emails. But there's little hard evidence that the Russians were behind the hack. Cyber-expert Bill Blunden wrote to me this morning: "Note that Julian Assange has said: 'We have not disclosed our source, and of course, this is a diversion that's being pushed by the Hillary Clinton campaign.'

"Thanks to documents released by Ed Snowden, and other whistleblowers, it's part of the public record that intelligence services have invested heavily in tools that are designed to subvert the process of attribution. It would be risky to presume that such activities were limited to the NSA and GCHQ. Likewise classified programs like JTRIG and HACIENDA are conducted with the explicit intention of obscuring the source of cyber intrusions. Entities from the private sector are also involved in this sort of activity.

"When dealing with an organization with the requisite skill and resources, successful attribution is highly unlikely. Subtle operational signatures can be mimicked and telltale forensic clues can be counterfeited. Welcome to the wilderness of mirrors. Peace, Bill."

¶ Sanders spent the morning sternly lecturing his rebellious delegation. He warned them not to bolt the Democrats for the Green Party. This is how Bernie repays Jill Stein's kindness in offering him her spot on the Green ticket. This was met by jeers and boos, as Bernie the Used Car Salesman was rebuked by his own cohort once again. They still ain't buying the lemon he's selling.

¶ What's this? Anthony Weiner is now giving testimonials for Hillary? How can she possibly lose? (I thought Huma had him on home detention. Someone check Weiner's Instagram photos tonight.)

¶ David Swanson writes in *CounterPunch* that the DNC is now less popular than atheism. After today's spectacle, the Satanists will be gaining on them fast.

¶ Jesse Jackson sent me his column this morning. It's a dispiriting piece of writing. Few people could have a better understanding of how an insurgent movement like the one Sanders led was sabotaged by the party establishment. The Democrats screwed Jackson twice. Yet Jackson writes that Hillary is the "clear choice" for president. Not the "necessary choice" or the "lesser evil." But the "clear choice." This, even though Bill Clinton has repeatedly race-baited Jackson. That's a strange kind of loyalty.

❡ Speaking of Hillary's "life-long commitment to children," very excited to hear the remarks of infamous child-killer Madeleine Albright tonight…

❡ If only the Sandernistas had the guts to boo that artifact of the Red Scare Era (which has never really ended), the Pledge of Allegiance. On its face it is an insult to the Constitution and trashes the values it claims to venerate.

❡ Here comes Chairwoman Marcia Fudge on the stage with her gavel again. Hammers it on the podium. Gets shouted down once again! Shuffles off shaking her head….

❡ Bernie should have negotiated to get Tulsi Gabbard a keynote speech in prime time, since she's about as close as the Democrats are likely to come to someone who will speak out against interventionist wars. I bet we go through the entire convention without hearing one word about drone strikes.

❡ Sanders delegate Shyla Nelson has moved Bernie to tears! To misquote Tom Hanks from *A League of Their Own*: "There's no crying in Revolutions, Bernie!"

❡ Senator Barbara Mikulski apparently didn't get the memo that "brother" Democrats and "sister" Democrats no longer covers all the bases.

❡ Deb Haaland, the first Native American chair of any state party, had the best line of the day so far when she introduced New Mexico's vote: "I'm proud to be from New Mexico, where our state question is: Red or Green? … Chile that is."

❡ The dilated and euphoric Oregon delegation seems to have spent their afternoon consuming edibles of unknown origin.

❡ Great to see the Puerto Rico delegation holding up "Free Oscar Lopez Rivera" t-shirts. Maybe Obama was tuning in, instead of playing golf. Perhaps he will even take action to finally right this lingering injustice. The South Dakota delegation put Hillary over the top. Too bad the delegation didn't take that opportunity to call for the pardoning of Leonard Peltier.

❡ At 6:53 EST, Bernie wiped out all of his delegates' votes. Sandernistas, you have now officially cast your votes for HILLARY CLINTON. Now you can really cry.

❡ So you find yourself suddenly transformed by Bernie's procedural magic wand from a Sandernista into a Clintonoid and the first face that you see upon awakening to this grim new reality is that of... political grifter extraordinaire Terry McAuliffe. Earlier in the evening, he told reporters what everyone else already knew: Hillary was going to "flip on the TPP." Get used to it. It will only get worse from here on out. Here comes Nancy Pelosi!

❡ It's surely an ominous sign for Hillary Clinton that the loudest applause of the Democratic Convention will almost certainly be for the forced surrender of Bernie Sanders and the public humiliation of his delegates.

❡ The cognitive dissonance of this convention is at max volume. How else can you explain how demurely Sanders just delivered his movement to the machine that represents everything he was allegedly waging war against: bailing out the banks, destruction of Glass-Steagall, fracking on a global scale, abandonment of organized labor, trade pacts from NAFTA to WTO to TPP, the death penalty, continuation of the drug war, the gutting of welfare, interventionist wars from Iraq to Syria, fealty to Wall Street money, vindictive and racist criminal justice policies, inaction on climate change, and blind loyalty to Israel.

❡ Most of the Sandernistas walked out after Bernie transferred (without consent) their votes to Hillary and had a sit-in outside of the convention center, where nobody saw them or cared. What kind of civil disobedience is that? Why not protest *inside* the hall, where the cameras are and the action is? A last blown opportunity to shake the establishment.

❡ Chuck Schumer just said that "when Hillary tells you something you can take it to the bank." Would that be Citibank or Goldman Sachs? Schumer was followed on the stage by Elizabeth Banks. I am not making this up.

❡ It was good to see Jimmy Carter looking so fit after his brain cancer. Too bad they didn't let him talk about Palestine and the Last Apartheid state, which would risk exposing the real fissures in his supposedly "unified" party.

❡ Every time a politician closed their remarks with "God Bless America" another bit of the Constitution died. This obnoxious tradition, which has infected politicians on the Left and the Right, has become a homegrown version of the dreaded Sharia Law.

❡ Eric Holder prefaced his remarks on criminal justice reform by arguing that the police need to be better armed. With what? Guided missiles and drones? Hillary Clinton's pimping for her husband's vicious Crime Bill by labeling young black men "super-predators" seems to have been wiped from the institutional memory of the Democrats. The drug war will be retooled, with opiate users the new villains.

❡ Holder swears that Hillary Clinton will be a champion of voting rights. This must come as a shock to the hundreds of thousands of potential Sanders voters who found their polling places mysteriously moved or closed, their ballots destroyed, or their votes not counted.

❡ I confess. In a tear-stained convention, I misted up during the testimonials of the Mothers of the Murdered, especially when

Travyon Martin's mother said that she was "an unwilling participant in this movement. I would not have signed up for this. I'm here today for my son, Trayvon Martin, who's in heaven." Too bad this heavy ceremony was diluted and demeaned by giving an hour to the Incarcerator-in-Chief, Bill Clinton, whose Crime Bill put 100,000 new cops on the streets. Since the passage of that infamous law in 1994, police have killed at least 20,460 civilians.

¶ Taser me when Lena Dunham's stopped talking.

¶ Skip that. Taser me when Barbara Boxer stops sputtering clichés.

¶ Did Rudy Giuliani co-produce the Dems' 9/11 video? The fact that they've brought up a NYPD detective, instead of a fireman or EMT worker, suggests that the DNC is compensating for the time they devoted to the Mothers of the Murdered.

¶ 15 years later and 9/11 remains a go-to political tripwire, shamelessly exploited by both parties. That fatal day has become sacralized—what Mircea Eliade called a hierophany, a sacrificial moment programed to flash across the profane world of politics. It's trotted out again here, by Hillary's surrogates, as an invocation to "defeat and destroy ISIS." Sound familiar?

¶ What's with Howard Dean? He can barely read the teleprompter. Did he share a joint with Lincoln Chafee backstage?

¶ Note to Hillary: You didn't bring about the ceasefire in Gaza. The bombing stopped after the Israelis ran out of targets, after having destroyed 70 percent of the structures in that narrow strip of defenseless land.

¶ So it's all about making women and girls more secure, is it? How many women and girls have been killed in Hillary's wars in Libya, Honduras, Syria, Iraq, Somalia, Yemen, Afghanistan, and Pakistan? Probably in the tens of thousands. So cheer up. Her body count is about 400,000 lower than Madeleine Albright's. But give her 8 years and she may yet catch up.

❡ Here comes Albright. Someone serve her an arrest warrant! *Lock her up! Lock her up!* Albright's sanctions on Iraq led to the deaths of a half-million Iraqi children. When asked by Leslie Stahl whether this death toll bothered her, whether the price was worth it, Albright didn't hesitate: "We think the price was worth it." She must be the world's most evil grandmother.

Typically, Albright began by invoking the Red Scare, moved on to praising Harry "A-Bomb" Truman and ended by demonizing Putin. The Cold War lives.

❡ Shouldn't Wellesley College lose its accreditation having matriculated both Albright *and* Clinton?

❡ What an odd short film trying to sell everything that Bill Clinton (Madeleine Albright's student) did for poor people, but neglecting to mention his destruction of welfare. Some of these people called themselves Clinton Babies? It's possible, of course, but did they all have paternity tests?

❡ Bill's creepy account of his courtship of Hillary at Yale makes him sound like a stalker.

❡ Does Bill have Parkinson's? Whole lotta shaking going on. Marc Solomon informs me that my diagnosis is off the mark. Solomon said Clinton is suffering from a drug reaction: "They've had him on Thorazine to shut him the fuck up during the campaign."

❡ Bill just can't help from making his speeches all about himself. More "I's" in Clinton's speech than in Trump's..

❡ Clintonian Revisionism: Bill now blames his defeat for reelection as governor on the Reagan landslide instead of his own hubris and incompetence.

❡ In Bill's tedious narrative of the Life and Times of the Clintons, there was sadly no mention of the only honorable member of the clan: Socks the Cat.

❡ Senator Warren is sitting in the Clinton box with Chelsea, cheering every banality uttered by Bill, even the whopper about how he "tried to bring peace and prosperity to America." Tell it to the people of Rwanda, Somalia, Iraq, Sudan and Serbia, President Bill. *Et tu, Elizabeth?*

❡ This being a family hour show, Bill was forced to redact several inconvenient chapters of his Scenes from a Marriage speech.

❡ According to Bill, you can take it from his friend Newt Gingrich that Hillary's "tough on national security." That seals it for me!

❡ The Clintons give Machiavelli a bad name. In fact, as my friend Jim Nicita says, "they make Machiavelli look like a Prince."

❡ Jane Fonda. Once she went to Hanoi to stop a war. Now she's appearing in a music video for a war criminal. Make it stop. I can't watch anymore.

❡ This whole night went off like a Neutron Bomb of Identity Politics, where the only ones left standing were demographic subsets and the Hedge Fund managers who fund the party. Is that all you've got? Doesn't that play right into Trump's trap? Or have I lost all political sense? The Democrats seem to have totally abandoned class politics. We are witnessing the complete triumph of neoliberalism.

Day Three: Night of the Hollow Men

❡ SINCE MY CO-EDITOR JOSHUA FRANK PREFERS TO GO SURFING rather than do his reportorial duty and watch the DNC Convention from gavel-to-gavel, he's telling me that I have to write another account of tonight's proceedings. I'm not sure I'm up to it 'frankly.' What would Hunter Thompson do? Oh, yes, he would get his body and mind in fighting form by having breakfast. I guess I'll follow the good Doctor's example: "Four Bloody Marys, two grapefruits, a pot of coffee, Rangoon crêpes, a half-pound of either sausage, bacon, or corned-beef hash with diced chilies, a Spanish omelette or eggs Benedict, a quart of milk, a chopped lemon for random seasoning, and something like a slice of key lime pie, two margaritas and six lines of the best cocaine for dessert." All to be consumed while naked. *Snarf! Sniff! Belch!* ALRIGHT! I'm primed. Bring on Biden!

❡ Margie Kidder was one of Hunter Thompson's best friends. I asked her if this menu remotely resembled his real appetites. Margie told me that she and Hunter were together during the 1984 Democratic Convention in San Francisco, where his main obsession was scoring some cocaine to get him juiced for covering the tedium of the convention.

"Here's what Hunter would do," Margie told me. "He believed firmly in getting your cocaine first, which at that convention involved spending a lot of time with a gay friend of mine he referred to in his writing as "the bowl of fruit". Then you got your drinks lined up and we would sit and watch the TV in the press room. I kept insisting in going out onto the floor to interview what often turned out to be ex-lovers of mine, who I couldn't really quote for obvious reasons. He was disgusted with me. At one point, back at the St Francis hotel, Hunter screamed down the hall at me "You are a political neophyte! You are a dangerous woman!" Then he went off to a party at Ann Getty's house or apartment and called her a fascist dyke and punched a hole in her living room wall and Pat Caddell (the Democratic pollster) and I had to race over with my trans driver Greta and our 1960s Cadillac convertible loaned to me by the gay community and rescue Hunter from the well-dressed and horrified Democrats. Senator Patrick Leahy thought he was funny. Few other Democrats did. But then Leahy often rode around with us in that Cadillac."

¶ Terry McAuliffe, the Clinton's former BFF (second now to Elizabeth Warren), mentor to Tim Kaine in the art of political grifting and current governor of Virginia, has an ego the size of Trump Tower. McAuliffe knows all of the Clinton's secrets. He knows what they think and how they deal. McAuliffe gave an early morning interview to *Politico*, where he confided to the reporter that Hillary was only pretending to oppose the TPP to neuter one of Bernie Sanders' main campaign themes. The governor assured the reporter that after the election Hillary would once again support the job-killing trade pact with a few cosmetic adjustments. The McAuliffe leak exposed the worst kept secret in Washington.

¶ Bill O'Reilly did his best last night to calm a perplexed nation, still reeling from Michelle Obama's allegation, which had not been vetted by the Texas School Book Commission, that slaves had built the White House. Yes, it's true, O'Reilly told his anxious viewers, but the slave construction workers were actually quite relaxed. In fact, they were "well-fed and had decent lodgings provided by the government." With these ameliorating words from a professional historian, Fox Nation slept soundly.

¶ A few days ago, Michael Moore hauled himself like a stranded walrus onto the set of the Bill Maher Show, where he predicted that Trump was going to win in the fall. Those of us who know Michael Moore knew that this was a con, a scare tactic to drive potential Greens, Libertarians or stay-at-home anarchists to vote for HRC.

Michael Moore does this every general election. Flirts with a Third Party candidate, then folds. He has previously confessed his obsession with Hillary, a mania with clear sexual overtones.

In his book, *Downsize This!*, Moore confessed his "forbidden love" for Hillary. He described her as "one hot shitkickin' feminist babe."

Now into my inbox lands a message from Moore under the subject heading: "Add Your Name?" How quaint, I thought. I didn't think we'd been on speaking terms since his deplorable betrayal of Nader in 2004. I was crushed to discover that this was actually a fundraising letter for MoveOn.org, imploring me to join with Moore and Lena *"friggin'"* Dunham to "do everything we can to stop Trump." Sicko, indeed.

¶ Trump is a carnival barker of bullshit. This morning at his press conference in Scranton he tweaked Clinton by calling on the infamous Russian hackers to release her emails. The reaction was seismic. Trump is inviting a foreign nation to spy on the US! Trump is calling for an enemy of the US to interfere in the American election! *Lions and tigers and bears, oh my!*

¶ The Democrats reacted with predictable hysterics, calling Trump's remarks "treasonous," which is ridiculous. What Trump actually said was that "if" Russia did in fact hack into Hillary's email account, then they should release the emails, especially the 30,000 emails that her lawyers deleted AFTER they were subpoenaed.

¶ Shortly after offending all of the foreign policy elites in both parties with his remarks on Russia, Trump broke with Republican orthodoxy again by announcing that he would support a $10 an hour minimum wage. Mike Pence, who opposes any minimum wage, must be having a hard time keeping up with the new talking points. The liberals, of course, reflexively denounced Trump's plan as "incoherent." But it is one more sign that Trump is trying to outflank Hillary on a range of issues. Fortunately for him, he doesn't have to veer his Rolls that far to get to the left of Clinton.

¶ The US is shocked! Shocked, I tell you!! That any government might want to interfere in US elections. It is morally wrong. It violates international law. It's the kind of action that violates every sacred principle of Democratic governments.

¶ In their quest to ensure a fully-informed American electorate, the Russian hackers should also release Trump's tax returns and the text of Hillary's Goldman Sachs speeches.

¶ The neoliberal ticket is now consecrated. The nomination of the unapologetically pro-fast track, pro-TPP Tim Kaine is approved without objection. Change (of positions) you can believe in. "At least he's not Putin," Jelle Versieren told me, "Nominating Putin would definitely be worse."

¶ Hillary's new BFF, Elizabeth Warren, refused to say whether Tim Kaine was the "right pick" for the Democratic Party. Instead Warren mumbled that Kaine "is a good man, he has a good heart, and he has a lot of experiences. I think he is going to be a valuable member of the team for Secretary Clinton and a valuable member of the team when she is president of the United States."

¶ New York Mayor Bill DeBlasio is now on stage. Wonder if he'll do a reprise of his "Colored Person Time" routine as a way to win back some of those Trump voters in western Pennsylvania?

¶ Bernie Sanders hasn't left the building with the Sandernistas. He gave a speech this morning to the Texas delegation, where he called Trump the "worst candidate in modern history." If that's true, then what are they scared of? The election should be a cakewalk.

¶ Almost every speaker on stage today has repeated the phrase "scary Donald Trump." They are working overtime to scrub away the eldritch image of Madeleine Albright from last evening, which must have given so many Democratic children a sleepless night.

¶ Jesse Jackson is a hollow shell of his former self. Once one of the most electrifying speakers of our time, he now is thoroughly pacified and house-trained. He can't really believe what he is saying about the woman who called black teenagers "super-predators"? What does he really mean when he says that you can "trust" the woman who pushed for the destruction of welfare that further impoverished the lives of poor black mothers and their children? "Hillary Time? Hope Time?" Jackson couldn't even look at the camera when he wrenched out those tortured phrases. If Jackson wasn't embarrassed for that speech, I was on his behalf. Once he was a rebel against the System. Now he is a hired gun for the elites.

¶ Who is up for a drinking game during Tim Kaine's speech!? One shot of mezcal for every formerly long-held position that Kaine reverses himself on tonight. If you don't pass out, then congratulations, you are probably one of Hunter Thompson's illegitimate children…

¶ The Clinton campaign is saturating the airwaves with a commercial featuring a montage of some of Trump's most offensive remarks while shocked children look on. In fact, most children probably watched few if any of Trump's heroniop before they saw all of them at once in Hillary's commercial. Is it really about protecting the kids, Hillary?

¶ Harry Reid and his wife just shuffled on stage wearing sunglasses they must have picked up at the House of Blues in Vegas. This is probably the last time we'll see Harry Reid at one of these things. I like Harry Reid. I don't know why. If I thought hard about it, I probably wouldn't. But I do. He's a former boxer and is still a fighter, even if he often punches the wrong targets. Alex and I interviewed him about 10 years ago. He was totally unpolished and unvarnished. We could have been talking to somebody in a bar. In fact, we were talking to somebody in a bar. Reid stood up to the nuclear lobby and won. He single-handedly kept nuclear waste out of Yucca Mountain. You won't see his kind in the future Democratic Party of pre-packaged *Westworld*-like clones.

¶ The ambitious Lt. Gov. of California Gavin Newsom just praised the "sunny optimism" of Ronald Reagan, specifically referencing the Gipper's "tear down that Wall" speech, one of the most rabid rants of the Cold War era.

¶ The Boho Gov. of California Jerry Brown, proponent of fracking and oil drilling, is the person the DNC picks to speak about climate change? Is Bill McKibben committing seppuku? One fracker endorsing the environmental *bona fides* of a ticket made up of two frackers. Give them points for consistency. Is Brown auditioning for Secretary of Interior or the board of Exxon. Is there a difference?

Why did the Democrats feel as if they could send out Jerry Brown to talk about global warming? Because Gang Green is already "all in" for Hillary and if the DNC thought they could stick this pro-oil hack right in their face with impunity, they'd be right…

¶ This gun violence sequence is unfolding like a flashback to Death Night at the Republican convention.

¶ There's Chief Charles Ramsey, the former police commissioner for Washington, DC, talking about gun violence and the "war on cops." You remember Ramsey don't you? He's the man who instituted traffic checkpoints in largely black sections of DC. Information on detained motorists who were committing crimes was then entered into a mass police database. Ramsey also ordered the illegal mass arrests of more than 700 protesters (perhaps even one of *you*) in Pershing Park during the World Bank and IMF protests in 2000. The city of DC was ordered to pay more than $8 million in fines as compensation for this trampling of civil rights. So much for the Constitution. Perhaps Hillary is auditioning Ramsey for the next Secretary of Homeland Security. Feel more secure?

¶ Cpt. Mark Kelly, Space Cowboy, just praised the "awesome extent of American power and capability" that engineered the overthrow of Saddam Hussein. The Democrats are doubling down on the Iraq War.

¶ Naturally, Commander Kelly's homily on the Iraq War is followed by a group-sing of 'What the World Needs Now' as a statement against gun violence! Maybe Yoko denied them the rights to 'Give Peace a Chance?' No matter which way you turn, people are living in an Alt Reality.

❡ In a strange cinematic interlude, the big screen behind the stage just aired a surreal film warning that Trump couldn't be trusted with the "nuclear button", which was partially narrated by… the nuclear bomber himself, Harry Truman!

❡ Leon Panetta, the CIA's master of drones, is being shouted down with "No war, No drone" chants, most of them coming from the Oregon and Washington state delegations. Play on, Sandernistas!

❡ Leon Panetta sniveling about Russian hacking is the best laugh of the night. Didn't his own hackers, working with their cohorts in Mossad, unleash the malicious Stuxnet worm on Iran?

❡ The floor managers are in crisis mode. They have given all of the delegates on the floor "Stronger America" placards, which they are waving with patriotic vigor as they shout "USA! USA!" to drown out the anti-war protesters. Did they import these people from the Trump rally in Scranton? They cut the lights on the anti-war protesters' section, who have responded with their Flashlight apps on their cellphones. Be prepared people!

❡ Are they arresting and waterboarding the protesters in the Oregon and Washington delegations now before Biden and Obama speak? Please text home!

❡ Right on cue, Rachel Maddow denounced what another MS-DNC hack called the Lunatic Left for heckling Leon Panetta, director of the CIA's remote control killing program. "It made no sense," she said. Which means it must have been impeccably timed.

❡ And now an important message on decency, justice and morality by Joe Biden, the man who betrayed Anita Hill and wrote the Clinton Crime Bill.

❡ Did they run the Biden speech through the plagiarism software? They should make sure to use the UK edition.

❡ For the Democrats the only man on Earth scarier than Donald Trump is Vladimir Putin, who Biden seems to believe is the Dr. Moriarty of Moscow.

❡ Introducing Michael Bloomberg, to present the Billionaire Seal of Approval to Ms. Hillary Clinton!

❡ Bloomberg: "We don't need a bomb thrower as president." Apparently, we need another drone launcher, instead.

❡ Leave it to Bloomberg to give the most coherent indictment of Trump. There's no hate quite as pure as that between rival billionaires.

❡ Re: Lenny Kravitz: They seem to be alternating the Love Songs with the War Speeches.

❡ Get the mezcal out, here comes Citizen Kaine. Will he embrace his inner neoliberal? Or make a false confession about his sudden epiphanies on trade, bank regulation, the death penalty, abortion, and collective bargaining rights?

❡ Tim Kaine is off to a halting start. Perhaps they should have had Kaine on at 3 pm? He has a goofy quality that would be endearing in a TV weather personality.

❡ If Hillary and Kaine are elected, will Toni Morrison dub Kaine the first Hispanic VP because he spoke some snatches of Spanish tonight?

❡ Tim Kaine, the Jesuit Missionary, talked about witnessing the horrors of the Honduran dictatorship without mentioning that it and its death squads were entirely supported by the US government and that the same generals were put back into power in a coup supported by Hillary Clinton!

❡ Kaine looks like he honed his rhetorical chops by watching home videos of Mister Rogers' Neighborhood. Did the Clintons ever see him give a speech or did they just take Terry McAuliffe's word for it? No insult intended to the great Fred Rogers, of course.

❡ Kaine, the Wall Street bag man, quoting John McCain's economic advisor for the 2008 campaign as an expert witness is probably not the most compelling testimonial against Trump.

❡ Obama enters to the banal mewling of Bono! How apt. At least he didn't profane James Brown or Smokey Robinson. He can have Bono.

❡ Obama may have been impotent to stop the killing of the kids at Newtown or the church members in Charleston. But he had complete authority to stop the killing of children, doctors, nurses, and wedding parties in Yemen, Syria, Iraq, Pakistan and Afghanistan, targeted by his drone strikes.

❡ Optimism is the word from the O-Man, which means things must be much worse than we think.

❡ With a smile on his face, Obama claims "gay marriage" as a victory on his resume, even though he opposed it.

❡ Obama: "There are pockets of the country that never recovered from factory closings." Pockets? Those pockets are big enough to shoplift the Great Lakes.

❡ Now Obama is quoting Reagan. Truman and Reagan have been quoted more frequently than any other figures at this convention. In fact, Obama's speech is played in the key of Reagan. He has said that he sees himself as a "transitional figure" like, yes, Reagan. He has succeeded beyond his expectations.

❡ Obama just said Hillary has been caricatured by some on the Left. I assume he's referring to the jacket cover of Doug Henwood's deliciously vicious book, *My Turn*, featuring Sarah Sole's painting ("Red Gun") of a stern Hillary aiming a revolver right at the reader.

❡ Obama could sell Trump Steaks to a vegan.

❡ Obama swears that Hillary is the "most qualified person ever to run for president." Perhaps. But she's qualified in all the wrong areas.

❡ Exit to Stevie Wonder. When Hillary surprised Obama on stage, she had the look of love in her eyes, as if she had just jilted Bill for Barack. But then wouldn't you, after Bubba's creepy stalker speech last night?

This was a night dominated by the hollow men of the Democratic Party: Panetta, Kaine, Biden and Obama. Men who knew better, but did worse. The theme was liberal virility, strength, and managerial efficiency. Missing was any empathy for the homeless and the hungry, the poor and the downtrodden. It was a frontal embrace of the neoliberal order, a demonstration that the Democrats have the competency and toughness to manage the imperial order in a time of severe internal and external stress.

The last three hours weren't a full-throated repudiation of Sandersism so much as a casual dismissal, as if the core concerns to which Bernie's movement gave voice—the ravages of economic inequality—didn't even merit their attention. And Bernie sat passively in the imperial box seats with Jane squirming at his side, watching it all unfold.

Barack Obama possesses so many scintillating skills, perhaps more skills than any other political figure of the modern era. Yet he put those magical gifts to such meagre, timid and often brutal uses. What a waste.

His is the tragedy of a squandered presidency.

Day Four: She Stoops to Conquer

❡ First things first. I want to apologize to the Sandernistas for any impolite things I may have written about you in the past 10 months. I especially want to apologize to those of you who rose up after your leader abandoned you, after Bernie wiped out your votes and muted your voices, after he turned you over to the DNC's thuggish floor managers and security guards, after he sat passively as your brave chants of "No More Drones" were drowned out by the fascist war-cry of *"USA! USA!!"* I want to apologize for doubting your resolve. I want to apologize without qualification. You didn't cry when Bernie betrayed you. At least, not for long. You marched right back into the Wells Fargo Center intent on spoiling the party. You didn't sour on your ideals. You refused to be domesticated. You pissed on their carpet. You shouted down their war criminals. You made this squalid affair fun for a few precious hours. And that ain't bad. Somewhere Abbie Hoffman is cracking a smile (though perhaps not at the spectacle of Meryl Streep ripping off his American flag shirt for her wardrobe during her bewildering performance, an act so incoherent it made one long for the Absurdist theater of Clint Eastwood and his empty chair routine.)

❡ I woke up this morning with a hangover that has defied the usual remedies. Too much mezcal from the Kaine Drinking Game (See above). Too many hours of tedium, dread and bombast. For relief, I turned to the Holy Text itself, *Fear and Loathing: on the Campaign Trail '72* and drank in HTS's savage denunciation of lesser-evil voting:

> How many more of these goddam elections are we going to
> have to write off as lame but 'regrettably necessary' holding
> actions? And how many more of these stinking double-
> downer sideshows will we have to go through before we can
> get ourselves straight enough to put together some kind of

> national election that will give me at least the 20 million
> people I tend to agree with a chance to vote for something,
> instead of always being faced with that old familiar choice
> between the lesser of two evils? I understand, along with a lot
> of other people, that the big thing, this year, is Beating Nixon.
> But that was also the big thing, as I recall, twelve years ago in
> 1960—and as far as I can tell, we've gone from bad to worse
> to rotten since then, and the outlook is for more of the same.

Ah, I feel better now. Will someone please fax that to Professor Chomsky, the preeminent salesman for Lesser Evil voting?

¶ Trump took to Twitter early this morning, as his hair was being replastered into place, and denounced the All Star lineup at the Democratic Convention last night as an orgy of "empty rhetoric." He wasn't wrong. The whole affair had the feel of one of those rock concerts featuring bands from the 1970s. The first few phrases were thrilling, then it all started to fade away into a nostalgic stream of familiar hooks and licks you've heard a thousand times before on Classic Rock AM radio. All played very well with magnificent staging and a dazzling light show, yet utterly antiseptic. The curious Tim Kaine interlude was the lone exception. It was hard to tell if his performance was camp or kitsch.

¶ Here's another reason to like Harry Reid and lament his looming retirement from the Senate. Shortly after his speech at the Democratic Convention, Reid laid some wood on the DNC. He said he was appalled by the DNC's efforts to sabotage Bernie Sanders' campaign, saying "Sanders didn't get a fair deal." Reid was asked if the Democratic Party has a back-up plan if further damaging emails emerge that might cripple Clinton. He shrugged his shoulders and said flatly, "No." Then again maybe Bernie deserved his fate. After all, he went along with the crushing of his campaign willingly enough, kind of like Al Gore did in 2000 when he refused to challenge his own stolen election. Bernie basked in the spotlight of his great betrayal, a surrender marketed as "unity." He savored each small, patronizing mention of his name last night by Kaine, Biden and Obama. Meanwhile, Sanders capitulated to demands from the DNC that he agree to prohibit one of his most ardent support-ers, Nina Turner, the black former state senator from Ohio, from appearing on stage to place his name in nomination. "If it were Beyoncé," Susan Sarandon fumed, "they would've made it work." It's even worse than that, Susan. The DNC is giving prime time slots on the stage to lesser talents than Beyoncé, including Carole King and Katy Perry. Turner's crime? She's refused to kneel down and endorse Clinton. Bernie's crime? He chose Hillary over Nina Turner. I tell you again: there's a reason so many blacks were suspicious about Sanders from the very beginning.

❡ The *New York Times* reports that after spending most of the spring in hiding, mega-donors are flocking back to the Clinton campaign. With Bernie vanquished and pacified, it is now safe for the powerbrokers of the Clinton cash machine to re-emerge, after being asked by the campaign to be discreet during the primaries. Now hedge funders, insurance execs, Big Pharma lobbyists and securities traders can get back to the business of wining and dining the Clinton team with style. Don't worry though. This is their last hurrah, before Hillary, you know, overturns *Citizens United* and slams shut the access door on them permanently *(wink, wink)*...

❡ Ned Sublette, author of the monumental *American Slave Coast*, writes to remind me that Bill Clinton did a 180 on Cuba policy. He campaigned on a pledge to normalize relations with Cuba, and then in 1996 did the opposite when he signed the vicious Helms-Burton Act, which tightened the embargo on Cuba nearly to the point of strangulation. The man who prodded Clinton to do so? Leon Panetta. Hit the replay button and shout him down again, in Spanish this time.

❡ We will no doubt be bombarded tonight with a cluster bomb of references to Hillary's brittle little book, *It Takes a Village*, which Cockburn savagely reviewed in *The Nation*, earning him a raft of rebukes from the imperial 'feminist' lobby. Here's a nugget that sums up the Clintonian approach to the exploitation of children for their political advantage:

"The Clintonite passion for talking about children as 'investments' tells the whole story. Managed capitalism (progressivism's ideal, minted in the Teddy Roosevelt era) needs regulation, and just as the stock market requires—somewhat theoretically these days—the Security and Exchange Commission, so too does the social investment (a child) require social workers, shrinks, guidance counselors and the whole vast army of the helping professions, to make sure the investment yields a respectable rate of return.

"The do-good progressives at the start of the century saw the family—particularly the immigrant family—as a conservative institution. So, they attacked it. Then their preferred economic system—consumer capitalism—began to sunder under the social fabric, and so today's do-gooders say that the family and the children, our 'investment,' must be saved by any means necessary. When the FBI was getting ready to incinerate the Branch Davidians they told Janet Reno the group's children were being abused. Save them, she cried. They went at it and all, including the children, were burned alive."

It will come as no surprise to seasoned Clintonologists that Hillary didn't actually *write* the book herself. It may, but shouldn't, come as a surprise that Hillary (like Trump) stiffed the ghost-writer of *It Takes a Village* out of the final payment. For the gory details, see Doug Henwood's book *My Turn*.

¶ Chuck Schumer: "I'm not worried about the white working class voters. For every blue collar white male we lose, we'll gain two college-educated women voters in the suburbs." I'd put my money on the TPP passing before Christmas.

What else would you expect from Schumer? The only regular interaction he has with working class people is with the elevator operator at Citibank when he rides up to the executive suite to pick up a campaign check.

I'll give Schumer this much: Though the Senator looks a little awkward, he must be a remarkable athlete: All these years racing from one TV camera to the next and not even a sprained ankle.

❡ I used to admire Laurence Tribe. I don't remember why now. I have a vague memory of him as a fierce defender of free speech and civil liberties. But here he is serving as a Clinton attack dog for the red-baiting of Donald Trump. In lockstep with the National Security elites, Tribe ludicrously said Trump's snarky remarks asking Russia to return Hillary's missing emails may have violated US law. If so, then you'd expect someone like Tribe to rush off to court to have such a law stricken down as unconstitutional. He knows it's all bullshit, but is apparently happy to play his role in the new McCarthyism. Perhaps Tribe thinks he's finally going to land on the Supreme Court. I'd support a Rand Paul-led filibuster against him. Have you no shame, professor?

❡ Expect some flood warnings as the tears begin to flow when the nation celebrates its own enlightenment in finally nominating a woman for president. The rest of the world will view this "historic moment" as something of a participation trophy. Eighty-five women from 54 different nations have already been elected or appointed as heads of government, starting in 1960 with Sirimavo Bandaranaike of Ceylon (Sri Lanka). Women have led governments in: India, Israel, Central African Republic, UK, Portugal, Dominica, Norway, Pakistan, Lithuania, Bangladesh, France, Poland, Turkey, Canada, Burundi, Rwanda, Bulgaria, Haiti, Guyana, New Zealand, Mongolia, Northern Cyprus, Senegal, South Korea, Sao Tome and Principe, Finland, Peru, Mozambique, Macedonia, Ukraine, Liberia, Bahamas, Germany, Jamaica, Moldova, Iceland, Croatia, Madagascar, Trinidad and Tobago, Australia, Slovakia, Mali, Thailand, Denmark, the Philippines, Guinea-Bissau, Slovenia, Latvia, Transnistria, Namibia, Greece, and Myanmar.

❡ Terry O'Neill, head of NOW, was asked about the tardiness of the US in relation to the rest of the world in electing a female head of state. Her response was a strange, almost misogynistic putdown of other women world leaders: "Many of them weren't feminists. Hillary was a born feminist. It was a harder road for her." *USA! USA!!!*

If Elizabeth Dole or Sarah Palin had somehow been elected president, I wonder if NOW would have put an asterisk by their names?

¶ Working class hero Sherrod Brown, the Ohio senator who was snubbed for the VP slot, told CNN that: "We're going to win in part by showing that Trump is a hypocrite on trade." Did he run this message by Hillary and Kaine?

¶ So far it's 6 for 6. 6 speakers, 6 "God Bless Americas." There goes Tammy Duckworth. Make that 7 for 7. Despite the allegation by Ben Carson that Hillary communes with Lucifer, it's looking like it will be another big night for God.

¶ Here comes Elizabeth Warren to give yet another testimonial to her new BFF, HRC: "Hillary is a fighter who never gives up for the people who need her most." Like Goldman Sachs, Monsanto and Benjamin Netanyahu. And you can take that to the bank.

¶ Joaquin Castro, the rising political star from Texas, is now on stage talking about how sensitive Hillary is to the plight of Mexican immigrants and undocumented aliens. This wasn't always the case and I highly doubt that it is now. During the NAFTA debates, the Clinton administration came down hard on the perils of Mexican immigration, using language that Trump may have cribbed. Al Gore even went so far as to blame Mexican immigrants for the spread of Satanic child abuse in the US. This was a double lie. First, Mexican immigrants weren't practicing Satanic abuse (or Santeria, as the Clinton people also alleged). And second, there was NO Satanic abuse epidemic. It is hard to document even a single real case. But these pernicious and racist lies helped sell the trade deal that continues to debilitate people on both sides of the border.

Remember that Hillary strongly backed the cruel Obama administration policy of rounding up thousands of immigrant children and sending them back to Mexico, El Salvador and Honduras? When Sanders confronted her once or twice, she essentially pulled a Madeleine Albright and said it was the right thing to do. All for the children, well, you understand…

¶ Chris Cuomo is giving a tribute to his father Mario Cuomo, both of whom worked as lawyers for… Donald Trump. The Trumps and Cuomos go way back. In fact, Donald encouraged Mario to run for president in 1988 (he hated Bush) and Mario urged Donald to run for governor of NY, after he stepped down. Bipartisanship you can believe in. (See Wayne Barrett's *Trump: the Deals and the Downfall*)

Cuomo is attacking Trump for "selling fear," as he simultaneously sells fear of Trump. The Republicans sell a dark dystopian fear, while the Democrats sell fear with a smile and a drone strike.

¶ Melania Trump's petty crime of word theft was much less noxious than the Democrats flagrant cribbing of the GOP's rabid *USA! USA!!* chants.

¶ Nancy Pelosi, defender of the poor & alleged inside stock (Visa) trader. Net Worth: $58 million. Who says West Coast liberalism doesn't pay?

Pelosi mumbles unintelligible syllables into the microphone for five minutes and flies off to check her portfolio to Wagner's "Ride of the Valkyries."

¶ Ted Danson and Mary Steenburgen have shown up to talk about how Hillary practices the "poetry of doing." Doing what, one might ask? Steenburgen, a native Arkansan, is the woman Bill Clinton reportedly took out to dinner the night he executed the brain-damaged Ricky Ray Rector to boost his poll numbers in the 1992 campaign. It's one thing to mock the disabled; it's something else entirely to put them to death for your own political advancement. There's ice running through those Clinton veins.

❡ Have the speakers tonight been instructed to be boring in order to make Hillary seem livelier by contrast? Or are they just flatline boring by nature?

❡ I said last night that Obama's speech was written in the key of Reagan. Now here is one of Reagan's speechwriters, Doug Elmets, giving a full-throated & unconditional endorsement of Clinton as the true heir of the Reagan legacy. Can anyone prove him wrong?

❡ Yet another cop at the mic, a moment of silence for the fallen police and speeches from relatives of dead officers. The Democrats have featured more cops as prime time speakers than the GOP, all of them lecturing about how "violence isn't the solution" to anything. Since January 1 of this year, 668 civilians have been killed by police.

❡ DNC Convention Motto for Coronation Night: "God, The Flag, and Drones." There seem to be more flags in the hall tonight than at Arlington Cemetery on Memorial Day. Curiously, despite the non-step odes to the dead, none are being waved at half-staff. Thanks for the memories…

❡ Rev. William Barber: "Jesus, a brown-skinned, Palestinian Jew…" Can't wait to see how Bill O'Reilly explicates that tomorrow night.

Whoops, he said "Palestinian" again! They may have to pull Rev. Barber off the stage to keep him from saying it another time. By special order of the convention rules, Palestinians are only allowed two mentions for the week.

❡ The chants of *USA, USA!!* during Khizr Khan's moving and powerful speech about his slain son is revolting. Do you have to be a "patriotic" American Muslim to enjoy the rights of the constitution that Khan showed? If you are a "patriotic Pakistani" does that protect you from a CIA drone strike?

❡ Gen. John Allen's deranged speech could have been written by Donald Rumsfeld. Perhaps it was. I feel like I've just watched the first 45 minutes of *Full-Metal Jacket* again.

❡ Trump has really gotten under the skin of the military-security establishment. His repeated swipes at NATO did it. They've united behind HRC. You've got to give him that. On the other hand, it gives an ominous new meaning to "Stronger Together."

❡ Who knew the Democratic National Convention would turn into a military recruitment video?

❡ How can they possibly top this? A live drone strike on the big screen?

❡ Two parties, both proto-fascist. How to choose?

❡ If I were the Iranians and North Koreans, I'd be hardening my bunk-ers, pronto. Assad should probably book a room at the nearest Ecuadoran Embassy.

❡ Gen. Allen just annihilated every humane sentiment expressed in Rev. Barber's powerful sermon. Perhaps that was the point.

❡ We begin to see the outlines of Hillary's economic plan: Military Keynesianism.

❡ Bernie, how do you like your party now?

❡ I wouldn't be shocked if those super-charged delegates goose-step out of the Wells Fargo Center tonight to invade Delaware, waving their flags and chanting *USA, USA!!!* all the way to Dover.

❡ Boomer, our Australian Shepherd, still hasn't emerged from the closet where he fled during Gen. Allen's war rant. Who can blame him?

❡ Hillary has already out-Thatchered the Iron Lady and she hasn't even been elected yet. She's made the complete metamorphosis from a Goldwater girl to a McGovern woman to a Reagan granny.

❡ Mission Impossible: Chelsea trying to humanize her mother after the blood-thirsty madness of the previous 30 minutes.

❡ Chelsea says her mother lost the fight for "universal health care." Not true. Her plan wasn't for "universal health care", but for another market-oriented scheme called "Managed Competition" and she fucked up that through her own incompetence and hubris, setting back the single-payer cause by at least a generation. No wonder Chelsea decided not to go to med school.

❡ "How many times will she leave her mark? How many ways will she light up the world?," the disembodied voice of Morgan Freeman asks. Well, how many drones and cruise missiles can Lockheed and Boeing manufacture in four years?

❡ The word of the night is *fight, fight, fight, fight, fight*. I don't know if the children are scared, but I am.

❡ I am Woman, hear my missiles ROAR!

❡ People in the audience are crying. I'm crying. I don't think we're crying for the same reasons.

❡ Hillary looks and sounds more and more like Cersei Lannister with each new speech.

❡ Hillary once again embraces Reagan to bash Trump. Reagan left the Democratic Party in the 1950s, but the Party apparently never left him.

❡ I'm getting a weird vibe that they might actually bring out Qaddafi's head on a pike.

❡ HRC says the "service part" always came more naturally to her than the "public part". Well, that explains the private email server…

❡ In her brisk recitation of the Rodham family history, Hillary somehow left out the fact that her father was a John Bircher. Of course, by the end of Hillary's second term her father may seem as meek as George McGovern.

❡ Does Hillary cough every time she lies, or does she cough every time she stumbles into the truth?

❡ Note the repeated emphasis on "believe" instead of "know" in Hillary's description of her political ideology. My friend John Trudell used to warn against the "believers." "Think more, believe less" he said. In Hillary's case, "believe" is likely shorthand for "make-believe."

❡ The comparisons of HRC to Lady Macbeth are grossly unfair to Lady Macbeth. Lady Macbeth had a conscience.

❡ She says she loves to talk about her "plans." Has she started yet? I haven't heard one specific plan. Maybe she's talking about her invasion plans. Oh, yes, she is getting around to that now…

❡ Pledge fealty to Israel. *Check.*
Defend NATO. *Check.*
Bash Russia. *Check.*
Destroy ISIS (by funding Al-Qaeda?). *Check.*
Praise the Generals. *Check.*
Hail our military (and its defense contractors) as a national treasure. *Check.*
Salute the troops. *Check.*
America is great. *Check.*
America is good. *Check.*
America is not a bully. *Check.*
Manifest Destiny. *Check.*
God bless America. *Check.*

❡ Unlike Hillary's idol Ronald Reagan, she gave no pledge to eliminate nuclear weapons, just a vow to have a more stable hand on the button than Trump. Like that Harry Truman. Duck and cover.

❡ How appropriate that it all ends with Hillary and Kaine standing before a golden (or is it Goldman?) shower raining down on America!

❡ As a final blessing, Hillary's preacher has come out to confirm at last what we've long suspected: there's a Methodism to her Madness.

❡ All Sandernistas should leave the Wells Fargo Center before they lock the exits. (See Red Wedding episode of Game of Thrones)

❡ Hillary passed her audition. She's the authentic Queen of Chaos and when she stoops, she stoops to conquer.

THE END,
OF OUR ELABORATE PLANS,
THE END

Bernie's Last Tape

[Bench. Lafayette Square. Winter. A light snow falls on the White House. An old man in a sleeping bag fiddles with a vintage cassette recorder. A pigeon alights on his shoulder. Shits. It is a sign. The man speaks.]

DID THEY CHEER ME ONCE? DID THEY?

So hard to tell.

The echoes are dim now. Fading.

People pass by and give me looks. Someone pitches a quarter and a couple of pennies. 27 cents. It was dollars once, wasn't it?

Don't they know me now?

Hearing has gone. Gone since the batteries died. Jane used to buy them. At Costco, was it? Not Wal-Mart. Never Wal-Mart.

I could never put them in. Big fat fingers, tiny little hearing machine. She had such nice hands. Jane. Small, delicate. Good for that kind of stuff.

Hearing is the first to go. Of the senses.

It warmed me once. Those cheers. On a cold night in Des Moines. Corn stubble covered with snow.

I could have won Iowa, they told me. Someone did. Later. Who, I don't know. Memory fades.

Something about missing ballots. Coin tosses. I should have objected, they said. Too late. Didn't want to make a fuss.

They pulled the same trick, time after time. Nevada. Missouri. Arizona.

But I did better than I hoped. Hope is what kills you. In the end.

At the beginning there was no hope. I was free then. Free to say what I wanted. Crazy old man, yelling at the banks. That's what they said. Some of them. I think.

I could say what they couldn't. What they thought. That's why they came. Maybe. To hear the crazy old man speak their thoughts. And people came. Out of nowhere. Madison. Portland, where that other bird came. Sparrow, propitious bird.

[Turns to pigeon.]

He didn't shit did he? Not on TV. Not like you.

Berkeley. Boulder. Masses of people. Young ones. Young women. Younger than Jane. Whiter than Jane. Most of them. My flock. All I had to do was whistle. They would come. Eager faces. Eager to please. Eager for revolt.

Even that Rachel at MS-DNC. She used to call every week. Seemed to like me. Once.

Later they turned on me. Like that Warren woman. Just when I was closing in, the knives came out.

Didn't they?

So hard to recall.

[Pause. Wipes away a tear or perhaps a flake of snow.]

It was the blacks who did me in. The blacks who never got me. The blacks who didn't vote. Why did they go for her, after all I did for them?

Getting arrested in Chicago. Marching with Dr. King. It was Dr. King, wasn't it? One of them. Wasn't there a photo?

The only time they came to my rallies was to interrupt me. Heckle me. To make demands. From me. Of all people. So ungrateful. Black Lives Matter. Of course, they do. But did that give them the right?

Yes, I voted for the Crime Bill. But I didn't call them Super-Predators, did I?

Rude. Unyielding.

Never build a movement like that. I tried to tell them. Ours was the *real* Revolution that would carry them, too.

Eventually. Patience.

They wouldn't listen.

Not like my Sandernistas. Someone called them that. The kids who came running when I called.

Was it all a joke?

[Pause. Closes his eyes. Broods.]

Ah, youth. You were my nectar.

Then came hope. Bitter, bitter hope.

That woman. The other, The woman with the pant suits, the Armani jackets and the Super Pac. She seemed invincible. Super Delegate Woman. I showed her. Didn't I? At the beginning.

My instincts. I should have trusted them. Base old instincts.

Not the Advisors. Where did they come from? The Advisors. Who sent them?

That first night. Under the lights. With the cameras rolling. Funny little Chaffee, down on the end. Had he been smoking weed? That's what someone whispered. I didn't smell it on him. Perhaps he vaped.

I miss him now. Silly little Lincoln. Town Car we called him. Old family. Small state. Spoke his mind. Not much on it. Still…

[Pause. Rummages in a garbage bag. Pulls out frayed photo of him hugging Hillary.]

Look at us. It all tumbles back now.

I had my chance. I could have taken her that night. I could have gone for the throat. Tiny little throat. Ripe for the slashing.

The question hangs before me even now. CNN. Clinton News Nitwits. That Anderson Cooper. TV trickster.

Why did I say it? It was scripted wasn't it? By whom? The question *and* the answer.

We knew it was coming. The one about the emails. They were her weakness. Stupid little emails. Stupid little answer.

Jane didn't like her. Never did. Go for the throat, Bernie. She said. Take her down. Take them all down, Bernie. Jane said.

Where is she now? Jane? With Chaffee? She saw something in me. Once. What was it?

Be above the fray, the Advisors said. Don't go negative. Preserve your image. Be chivalrous.

So I intervened. Came to her rescue. Made my pact, now can't turn back.

"The American people are sick of hearing about her damn emails!" Oh, the press loved it. I was the white knight.

It was over then. I didn't know it. Hillary did. She knew, dammit. That smirk. Walking dead. That's what Jane said. You blew it, Bernie.

But the polls, I said, look at the polls! I could have won. Should have won. There's some cold comfort. They can't take that away from me. The polls, the platform, the convention speech.

And the money. $220 million. Where did it all go?

If only I could have it all back. The fire. The children. Hope.

No, better this way. Better not to go on. Better not to hope.

> *[The old man hangs his head. The pigeon takes flight. The tape records only silence.]*

Gratis

MY HUMBLEST THANKS TO BECKY GRANT FOR HOLDING IT ALL together under pressure, Joshua Frank for co-piloting, Nathaniel St. Clair for spreading the word, Deva Wheeler for navigation, Martin Billheimer and Ruth Fowler for sharpening the sentences, Tiffany Wardle for the sensational design, and Kimberly Willson-St. Clair for her love, patience, knowledge and gravity. This book was written under the influences of Merle Haggard, Lemmy, Ornette Coleman, Prince, John Trudell and Clackamas Kush.

Index

2000 presidential election 29, 71, 92

A League of Their Own 75

Adorno, Theodor 47

Afghanistan War 22–3, 34–5, 58, 71–2, 78–9, 88–9

African-Americans 16–7, 48–9, 57, 68–9, 77, 105

Ailes, Roger 26

AIPAC 15–6

Alabama 25–6

Albright, Madeleine 72–4, 76–7, 84–5, 96–7

Alighieri, Dante 41

Allen, Gen. John 97–9

American Slave Coast 93

Anti-Semitism 31, 69–70

Anti-terrorism laws 16–7

Anti-war movement 13–4

Antoinette, Marie 31

Arizona 42

Arkansas 53

Art of Courtly Love (Capellanus) 29

Assange, Julian 65–6, 70

Assassination 2, 31–2

Atlanta, Georgia 53

Austin, Texas 49

Authorization for Use of Military Force (AUMF) 37, 51

Banks 2, 29, 49–50, 52–3, 76

Barber, Rev. William 97–8

Barrett, Wayne 25–6, 96

Barrow, Clyde 35

BBC 71

Beatles, The 1

Beckle, Bob 65–6

Being and Time (Heidegger) 45

Bell Curve (Murray) 48

Ben & Jerry's 48

Biden, Joe 69, 81, 86–7, 89, 92–3

Big Pharma 93–4

Bill Maher Show 82

Billheimer, Martin 111

Billionaires 2

Black Lives Matter (BLM) 3, 16, 59

Blinder, Alan 53–54

Blitzer, Wolf 33

Bloomberg, Michael 65, 87

Blunden, Bill 73–74

Bolivaran Revolution 21

Bono 88–9

Booker, Cory 69–70

Boxer, Barbara 77

Bradley, Bill 18–9

Branch Davidians 93–94

Brock, David 31

Bronson, Charles 30

Brown, James 88

Brown, Jerry 18–9, 85–6

Brown, Sherrod 95–6

Browne, Jackson 14

Burke, Edmund 71

Burlington Air Base 22

Burroughs, William 4–5

Bush, George HW 25, 54, 96–7

Bush, George W. 3, 37–8

Caceres, Berta 58–9

Caddell, Patrick 81–2

California primary 57

Cameron, David 33

Campaign finance 1, 58–9, 73–74, 91–2

Canova, Tim 65

Capellanus, Andreas 29

Carter, Jimmy 18, 59, 76–7

Carville, James 70

Castro, Joaquin 95–6

Catholicism 42–3

Central Intelligence Agency (CIA) 21, 37–9, 86–7, 97–8

Chafee, Lincoln 77–8, 107

Charleston, SC, massacre 88–9

Chavez, Hugo 21

Chicago, Ill. 50

Chisholm, Shirley 18–9

Chomsky, Noam 91–92

Citibank 54, 76, 94

Citizens United v. FEC 26, 91–2

Civil liberties 85–7

Clark, George 25

Cleveland, Ohio 66

Climate change 76, 85–6

Clinton, Bill 13–4, 16–8, 29–30, 38–40, 50, 51–53, 69, 71–2, 74–5, 78, 87, 88–92, 93–97

Clinton, Chelsea 79, 98–9

Clinton, Hillary 1, 3, 4–5, 15, 16–7, 29–2, 33–4, 47–9, 51–53, 63–4, 66–101, 106–8

CNN 33, 66, 95, 107

Coal industry 70–1

Cockburn, Alexander 18, 23, 31, 71, 85, 93

Cockburn, Andrew 22

Cold War 22, 34, 85–6

Coleman, Ornette 111

Colombia 30

Communism 31

Congressional Black Caucus (CBC) 29

Conspiracy theories 55

Cooper, Anderson 107

Corbyn, Jeremy 21

Correct the Record (PAC) 21
CounterPunch 64, 73–74
Credit derivatives 55–6
Creech Air Base 50–1
Crime Bill (of 1994) 16, 50–1, 58, 77, 84, 87, 106
Criminal justice reform 3, 50–1, 58, 76
Cruz, Ted 34–5
Cuba 93
Cuomo, Chris 96
Cuomo, Mario 18, 25, 96
Czech Republic 25
Danson, Ted 96–7
Danton, Georges 71
Davine, Tad 49–50
Dean, Howard 49–50, 77
Death penalty 42, 49–50, 76, 96–7
DeBlasio, Bill 84
Debord, Guy 26
Debt, consumer 2, 5
Democratic Leadership Council (DLC) 54–5
Democratic National Committee (DNC) 3–4, 6–8, 18, 30, 57–8, 65–6
Democratic National Convention 3–5, 65–101
Democratic Party 3–4, 6–8, 30, 39, 57–8, 65–6
Deportation, of immigrants 95–6
Dickens, Charles 6, 26
Divine Comedy (Dante) 41
DNC email hack 65–6, 70, 73–77, 81, 92–3, 94–5
Doctors Without Borders 22–3
Dole, Elizabeth 95

Downsize This! (Moore) 82
Dr. Faustus (Marlowe) 31
Drone warfare 2, 23–4, 50–1, 77–8, 86, 88, 91–2, 97
Drug war 70, 76–7
Drugstore Liberal, The (Sherrill) 22
Duckworth, Tammy 95
Dunham, Lena 77, 82
Eastwood, Clint 91
Economy 1–2, 3, 5, 7–8, 22, 51–53, 76, 83, 87, 93–4
Education 45–6
El Salvador 65, 96
Elmets, Doug 97
Erdogan, Recep 34
Estabrook, Carl 72
Executive compensation 51–52
ExxonMobil Corp. 86
Facebook 73
FALN 75
Fast Track trade authority 81–2
Fear and Loathing on the Campaign Trail 72 (Thompson) 91–2
Federal Bureau of Investigation (FBI) 93–94
Federal Reserve 51–52
Feminism 91–2
Flaherty, Patrick 70
Florida 65
Fonda, Jane 79
Foreclosure crisis 50–1
Foster, Jody 34
Fowler, Ruth 111
Fox News 26, 97
Fracking 50–1, 58, 70, 76
France 33
Frank, Barney 67
Frank, Joshua 65, 81, 111
Freeman, Morgan 98

Freiburg University 45
French Revolution 31, 71
Fudge, Marcia 67, 75
Futures market 53
Gabbard, Tulsi 75
Game of Thrones 99–100
GATT 30
Gay marriage 88–9
Gaza 77–8
Georgia 25–6
Getty, Ann 81–2
Gillibrand, Kirsten 68
Gingrich, Newt 79–80
Giuliani, Rudolph 77–8
Glass–Steagall Act (of 1933) 54–5
Global War on Terror 2, 22, 30–1, 33–4, 50–1, 76, 78–9, 86, 88–9
Goldman Prize 57
Goldman, Sachs 4, 17, 49–50, 53–54, 76–7, 81–2
Goldwater, Barry 5
Gore, Al 29, 71–2, 92, 95–6
Gore, Tipper 68, 71
Grand Hyatt Hotel (NYC) 25
Grant, Becky 65, 111
Great Britain 33
Great Depression 51–2
Great Lakes 88
Great Recession, (2007–9) 88–9
Great Society 7–8
Green Party 3–4, 19, 66–7, 74–5
Grenada, invasion of 69
Guevara, Ernesto "Che" 31
Gun control 22–3, 86–7
Haaland, Deb 75
Habeas Corpus 16
Hacking 65–6, 68–9, 71–72, 81–2, 86, 92, 94–5
Haggard, Merle 111

Hamilton, Alexander 55
Hanks, Tom 75
Harper's 22
Harvard Law School 42
Hay, Bruce 42
Health care 49–50, 58,
    98–9
Heidegger, Martin 45–6
Helms-Burton Act (of
    1996) 93
Henwood, Doug 71,
    88, 94
Hersh, Seymour 34–5
Hill, Anita 87
Hinkley, John 34
Hispanics 13, 57–8, 68–9
Hitchens, Christopher
    16
Hitler, Adolf 45–6
Hobbes, Thomas 7–8
Hoffman, Abbie 91–2
Holder, Eric 77
Homelessness 3, 89–90
Honduras 58–9, 68, 78,
    87–8, 96–7
Humphrey, Hubert H.
    15, 21–22, 31
Hunger 3, 89–90
Huntsville Unit Prison
    (Texas) 49–50
Hussein, Saddam 37–39,
    86
IMF, protests 85–7
Immigration policy 26,
    42–2, 95–7
Imperialism 18, 34–5, 58
Income tax 68–9
Insurance industry 58
Internal Revenue
    Service (IRS) 68
Iowa caucuses 31–2,
    105–6
Iran 13, 33–4, 86–7,
    98–9
Iran/contra scandal 13
Iraq Liberation Act (of
    1998) 37–8

Iraq War 3, 13–4, 16,
    30–2, 33–4, 49–50,
    76, 78, 86–7, 88–9
ISIS 32–4, 77, 99–100
Israel 15–6, 76, 77–81,
    87, 99–100
Israel lobby 15–6
It Takes a Village
    (Clinton) 69–70, 93
Jackson, Jesse 15, 74,
    84–5
Jaspers, Gertrude 45–6
Jaspers, Karl 45–6
Jeffords, James 13–4
John Birch Society
    99–100
Johnson, Gary 66–7
Judaism 31
Kagan, Elena 41
Kaine, Tim 66–7, 70,
    82, 83–84, 87–88, 89,
    92–3
Kardashian, Kim 57
Kelly, Mark 96–7
Keynon, John Maynard
    22
Keynesian economic
    theory 22
Khan, Khizr 97–8
Kidder, Margot 73–74,
    81–2
Kilmister, Lemmy 111
King, Carole 92–3
King, Martin Luther
    Jr. 106
Klamath River 65
Knowles, Beyoncé 92–3
Kosovo 30
Kravitz, Lenny 87
Kucinich, Dennis 18
Kunduz, Afghanistan
    (bombing of) 22–3
Labour Party (UK) 21
Lannister, Cersei 99–100
Las Vegas, Nev. 49–50,
    85
Lawrence v. Texas 42
Leahy, Patrick 22, 82–3

Lee, Barbara 49
Lehman Brothers 52
Lennon, John 1
Lesser Evil voting
    strategy 91–2
Libertarian Party 66–7,
    82–3
Libyan War 17, 34–5, 50,
    58–9, 78–9
Lieberman, Joseph 18
Lopez Rivera, Oscar
    75–6
Los Angeles, Cal. 71
Lovato, Demi 69
Machiavelli, Niccolo
    29–30, 79
Maddow, Rachel 17,
    86–7, 105
Madison, James 44
Magna Carta 16
Maher, Bill 82
Maples, Marla 25–6
Marley, Bob 50–1
Martin, Trayvon 77
McAuliffe, Terry 75–6,
    82, 88–9
McCain, John 90
McCarthy, Eugene 1,
    18–9
McCarthyism 31, 94–5
McCartney, Paul 1
McGovern, George
    18–9, 99–100
McKibben, Bill
    85 Interior Dept. 85
McLuhan, Marshall 69
Meet the Press 23
Methodism 51–2, 101–2
Mexico 26, 53–4
Microsoft Corp. 29
Mikulski, Barbara 75–6
Military bases, US 2
Minimum wage 83–4
Minnesota 22
Missouri primaries
    46, 101
Monaco 61
Mook, Robby 64

Moore, Michael 78
Morrison, Toni 83
Mossad 82
MoveOn.org 78
Mr. Rogers' Neighborhood 84
MS Windows 27
MS-NBC 15, 61–2, 82–3, 101
Murray, Charles 48–9
Nader, Ralph 19, 26–7, 29, 82–3
NAFTA 30, 55, 76–7, 95–7
Nation, The 93
National Economic Council (NEC) 54
National Guard 22
National Organization for Women (NOW) 95–6
National Security Agency (NSA) 73–74
NATO 34–5, 97–99, 99–100
Nazis 45–6
NBC News 68–9
Nelson, Shyla 75
Neoliberalism 18, 30–1, 50–1, 58–9, 79–80, 87–8
Nero, Emperor of Rome 27
Netanyahu, Benjamin 95–6
Nevada caucuses 48, 105
New Deal 7–8
New Hampshire primaries 29
New Mexico 74–5
New York primaries 1, 3–5
New York Times 14, 66, 70–1, 92–3
Newsome, Gavin 85–6
Newtown, Conn., massacre 88–9
Nicaragua 13–4

Nicaraguan Revolution 13–4
Nixon, Richard M. 91–4
North Korean 98–9
Nuclear waste 85–6
Nuclear weapons 2, 23, 49–50, 86–7, 99–100
NYPD 77–8
O'Malley, Martin 16–7
O'Neill, Terry 95–6
O'Reilly, Bill 82–3, 97
Obama, Barack 6–7, 17–8, 37–8, 41, 58, 66–7, 86–7, 89–90
Obama, Michelle 69–70, 82–3
ObamaCare 58–9
Occupy Wall Street movement 3–4
Oil & gas industry 21, 52, 58, 70–1, 76–7, 84–5
Only the Super-Rich Can Save Us! (Nader) 26
Ono, Yoko 86
Operation Desert Fox 37–8
Opiates 68–9, 77–9
Opus Dei sect 42–3
Order of St. Hubertus 43
Oregon 22–3, 75–6, 86–7
Oregon delegation 86–7
Organized labor 49–51, 58, 67, 76–7
Originalism, legal theory 42
Pakistan 78–9, 88–9, 97–8
Palestinians 76–7, 77–9, 97–9
Palin, Sarah 95–6
Panetta, Leon 86–7, 89–90, 93–4
Paris, France (terrorist attacks in) 34
Parker, Bonnie 35

Paul, Rand 94–5
Pawn shops 5
Pay day loans 5
Pelosi, Nancy 67–8, 76–7, 96–7
Peltier, Leonard 74–5
Pence, Mike 83–4
Perry, Katy 92–3
Pershing Park (DC) 85–6
Phenomenology 45–6
Philadelphia, Penn. 3–4, 65–101
Plagiarism 87–8
Pledge of Allegiance 74–5
Police 77–8, 85–7, 97–8
Police shootings 3, 16–7, 97–8
Political action committees (PAC) 1, 21
Political consultants 49–50, 57, 59, 107
Politico 57, 82–1
Populism 54–5
Post-Modernism 16
Poverty 3, 6–7, 89–90
Power, Samantha 41–2
Prince 111
Prisons 3, 52, 58, 68–9
Progressive Alliance 13
Progressive movement 93–4
Promontory Inter-financial Network 53–54
Prospect Park 1
Puerto Rico 75–6
Putin, Vladimir 34–5, 78–9, 83–85, 87–8
Qaddafi, Muammar 59–60, 99–100
Queen of Chaos (Johnstone) 37
Race-baiting, by Clintons 74–5

Rachel Maddow Show
17, 86–88, 105
Ramsey, Charles 85–6
Raqqa, Syria 35
Reagan, Ronald 13–4,
25–6, 78–9, 84–5,
88–9, 96–8, 99–100
Red-baiting 31
Rehnquist, William 41
Reid, Harry 84–6, 92–3
Reno, Janet 93–95
Republican National
Convention 66–7
Republican Party (GOP)
25, 33–4, 39–40, 66–7
Robespierre,
Maximilien 31
Robinson, Smokey 88–9
Rodham, Hugh 99–100
Rogers, Fred 88–9
Roosevelt, Theodore
93–4
Rose Law Firm 68–9
Roseburg, Oregon
(massacre at) 29–4
Rubin, Robert 54
Rubio, Marco 45–6
Russia 34–5, 55, 68–9,
73–75, 83–4, 87–8,
94–5, 99–100
Rwanda 79–80
Safeway 2
San Bernardino, Cal.
(terrorist attacks
in) 34
San Francisco, Cal. 81–3
Sanctions, against Iraq
37–8, 52, 58, 78–9
Sanders, Bernard New
York primaries 1,
3–4, 49–50, Super
Tuesday 3–4, 58,
Vermont 13, 15, 19–21,
Israel 15–6, Serbian
War 13–4, F-35 21–23,
Iowa caucuses 29–31,
New Hampshire
primary 29–30,

Syrian War 33–5, 37,
Iraq War 37–9, 52–3,
Wisconsin primary
47–8, DNC 47–8,
57–8, 66–5, Hispanic
voters 57–8, black
voters 16–7, 57–8,
106–7, California
primary 57–8, at
DNC convention
64–97, convention
speech 70–82
Sanders, Jane 89–90,
105–9
Santería (religion) 95–7
Sarandon, Susan 92–3
Satanic abuse, scare
95–6
Saudi Arabia 33–4
Saudi royal family 33
Scalia, Antonin 41–43
Schroeder, Patricia 18–9
Schumer, Charles 67,
76–7, 94–5
SEALS, Navy 2
Securities & Exchange
Commission (SEC)
93–4
September 11, 2001,
attacks of 21–22, 77–8
Serbian War 13–4, 16,
30, 37–9, 52, 79–80
Sherrill, Robert 21–22
Shia Muslims 33
Silverman, Sarah 69–70
Simon, Paul 69–70
Single-payer health care
51–2
Situationist
International 26
Slavery 82–3
Snapchat 59
Snowden, Edward 73–74
Socialism 13, 18–9
Socialist Party 19
Socks the Cat 79–80
Solomon, Marc 78
Somalia 78–79

South Carolina
primaries 17, 25
South Dakota 74–5
St. Clair, Nathaniel
65, 111
St. Francis Hotel (SF)
81–2
Stahl, Leslie 78–9
State Dept. 34–5, 68–9
Steenbergen, Mary 96–7
Stein, Dr. Jill 3–4, 66–8,
74–6
Stephanopoulos, George
23
Streep, Meryl 91–2
Stuxnet virus 86–7
Sublette, Ned 93–4
Suicides, military 35
Sunstein, Cass 41
Super delegates 48–9,
59–60, 107–8
Super Tuesday
primaries 3–4, 58
Super-PACS 1, 21, 54,
107
Supreme Court 41–42,
94–5
Swanson, David 74
Swift, Jonathan 41
Syrian War 21–22, 33–5,
37, 76–7, 88–9
Tea Party 3
Television City (NYC)
25
Texas 41, 43–4
Texas Schoolbook
Commission 82
Thatcher, Margaret 98–9
Therapy 68
Thomas, Clarence 42–3
Thompson, Hunter S.
81–2, 84–5, 91–3
Tomahawk cruise
missile 38
Torture 86–7
Trade pacts 4–5, 30,
58–9, 67–8, 75–7,
82–5, 94–5

Trans-Pacific
  Partnership (TPP)
  4–5, 67–8, 75–7,
  82–4, 94–5
Treasury Dept. 55
Tribe, Laurence 94–5
Trudell, John 99–100, 111
Truman, Harry S. 78–9,
  86–7, 88–9
*Trump: the Deals
  and the Downfall*
  (Barrett) 25–6, 96–7
Trump Steaks 88–9
Trump Tower 25, 82–3
Trump, Donald 4–5,
  6–8, 25–7, 42–3,
  45–7, 65–6, 68–9,
  78–9, 83–85, 87–8,
  92–3, 94–5, 96–7,
  97–101
Trump, Fred 25
Trump, Ivana 25–6
Trump, Melania 96–7
Turkey 34
Turner, Nina 92–3
Ukraine 16
Umpqua Community
  College 22–3
UN Human Rights
  Council 33
Unemployment 3, 89–91
United Nations (UN)
  33, 39
United Socialist Party of
  Venezuela 21
United Steelworkers
  Union 67–8
Venezuela 21, 68–9
Verizon 51
Vermont 7–8, 13, 15,
  22–3
Vermont Air National
  Guard 22–3
Versieren, Jelle 81
Vietnam War 21–2,
  79–80
Virginia 82–3
Vote rigging 57–8

Voter suppression
  59–60
Voting rights 77–8
Wahhabi sect 33
Wal-Mart 68–9
Wall Street 3, 29–30,
  53–55, 76–7, 88–9,
  93–4
Wardle, Tiffany 111
Warren, Elizabeth
  69–70, 79–80, 82–3,
  83–85, 95–6, 105–6
Washington delegation
  86–8
Washington Post 14
Wasserman Schultz,
  Debbie 59–60, 65–6,
  69–70
Waterboarding 86–7
Weekly Standard 41
Weiner, Anthony 74–5
Welfare reform 17, 76–7,
  78–9, 84–5
Wellesley College 78
Wellstone, Paul 18
Westworld 85
Wheeler, Deva 65, 111
Whistleblowers 73–75
White House, slave
  labor 82–3
Whitewater scandal 53
Whitney, Mike 71
Wikileaks 65–6, 68–9,
  73–5
Willson-St. Clair,
  Kimberly 111
Winooski 44 (group)
  13–4
Wonder, Stevie 88–9
World Bank, protests
  85–7
World of Warcraft
  (game) 59
WTO 30, 76–7
Yemen 16, 33–4, 58–9,
  78–9, 88–9
Yippies 91–2
Yucca Mountain 85–6

BERNIE & THE SANDERNISTAS

CPSIA information can be obtained
at www.ICGtesting.com
Printed in the USA
LVOW03s2155230118
563697LV00017B/2323/P